THE UNITED STATES AND LATIN AMERICA: SHAPING AN ELUSIVE FUTURE

Donald E. Schulz

March 2000

*****

*****

Special thanks are due Colonel Joseph Nuñez, General (ret.) Fred Woerner, Douglas Lovelace, Gabriel Marcella, Max Manwaring, and Richard Millett for their constructive comments and suggestions on an earlier draft. Needless to say, any errors of comission or omission are entirely the responsibility of the author.

*****

Comments pertaining to this report are invited and should be forwarded to: Director, Strategic Studies Institute, U.S. Army War College, 122 Forbes Ave., Carlisle, PA 17013-5244. Copies of this report may be obtained from the Publications and Production Office by calling commercial (717) 245-4133, FAX (717) 245-3820, or via the Internet at rummelr@awc.carlisle.army.mil

*****

Most 1993, 1994, and all later Strategic Studies Institute (SSI) monographs are available on the SSI Homepage for electronic dissemination. SSI's Homepage address is: http://carlisle-www.army .mil/usassi/welcome.htm

*****

The Strategic Studies Institute publishes a monthly e-mail newsletter to update the national security community on the research of our analysts, recent and forthcoming publications, and upcoming conferences sponsored by the Institute. Each newsletter also provides a strategic commentary by one of our research analysts. If you are interested in receiving this newsletter, please let us know by e-mail at outreach@awc.carlisle.army.mil or by calling (717) 245-3133.

ISBN 1-58487-016-8

FOREWORD

Developing a U.S. national security strategy for Latin America is a daunting task in an era of scarce resources. Yet, it is important at this historical juncture that the effort be undertaken. The demise of the Cold War has produced not an "End of History" but a "New World Disorder," which may well become more tumultuous in the decades ahead. Thus, it is crucial at this turn of the millennium to reconsider the prospects for regional security, the challenges that both new and old dangers may pose to U.S. interests, and the kind of strategy and policies that might enable the United States to both better cope with current problems and head off those that are just over the horizon.

In this report, Dr. Donald E. Schulz first analyzes U.S. security interests in Latin America. He then surveys the primary challenges to those interests, and how well U.S. strategy and policy are equipped to cope with them. But he does not stop there. He suggests how the security environment is likely to change over the next quarter century, both in terms of the new dangers that may arise and the evolution of problems that already exist. His conclusion that we are not strategically equipped to face the future is a disturbing one, for Latin America's importance to the United States is growing fast even as our attention is flagging. Will we have the insight to recognize our own interests, the will to commit sufficient resources to attain them, and the intellectual wherewithal to relate our means to our ends?

This is a timely study. U.S. presidential elections will be held later this year. Thus, this report provides a excellent opportunity for policymakers and aspiring policymakers alike to begin reviewing where we are and where we are going. The Strategic Studies Institute is pleased to publish this monograph as a contribution to what promises to be a lively debate over our Latin American policy.

DOUGLAS C. LOVELACE, JR.
Interim Director
Strategic Studies Institute

BIOGRAPHICAL SKETCH OF THE AUTHOR

DONALD E. SCHULZ is Chairman of the Political Science Department at Cleveland State University. Prior to that he was Research Professor of National Security Policy at the Strategic Studies Institute of the U.S. Army War College. Dr. Schulz has authored or edited a half dozen books, including *The Role of the Armed Forces in the Americas: Civil-Military Relations for the 21st Century*; *Mexico Faces the 21st Century*; *Cuba and the Future*; *The United States, Honduras and the Crisis in Central America*; *Revolution and Counterrevolution in Central America and the Caribbean*; and *Political Participation in Communist Systems*. His numerous articles have appeared in both scholarly and policy journals, including *Foreign Policy*, *Washington Quarterly*, *Orbis*, the *Journal of Interamerican Studies and World Affairs*, and *Mexican Studies/Estudios Mexicanos*, as well as media outlets such as *Newsweek*, the *Washington Post*, the *Miami Herald*, the *Los Angeles Times*, and the *Christian Science Monitor*. Currently, he is completing a book on "Narcopolitics in Mexico" and co-editing a volume on "War and Peace in Colombia."

THE UNITED STATES AND LATIN AMERICA: SHAPING AN ELUSIVE FUTURE

> The standard U.S. approach to security relations in the Western Hemisphere is at the end of an era. Deep and wide-spread changes in the hemisphere's political and economic environment over the last 20 years have introduced anomalies that the existing U.S. paradigm did not anticipate. Transformations in Latin America and the Caribbean since the Cold War have produced a growing sense that Washington's past experience is no longer adequate to meet problems shaped by an environment that it in part created. . . . The United States is moving in this security milieu without a clear view of the horizon or a plan of action to get there.
>
> John A. Cope[1]

The end of the Cold War has witnessed a major transformation of the international security environment. The Evil Empire is no more. Yet, early predictions that we were entering a "New World Order" have proven premature. The growing chaos in Russia, the Asian economic crisis, the bloodbaths in the Balkans and Central Africa, the U.S.-Iraq war, the spread of weapons of mass destruction, nonstate threats (e.g., from terrorists and drug mafias), and other dangers to international peace and stability suggest that, while the old order has changed, a new one has yet to emerge. In many respects, indeed, the current milieu bears as much resemblance to a "New World Disorder" as anything else.[2]

Latin America is no exception. While considerable progress has been made on some fronts—especially with regard to democratization and the adoption of market reforms—there has been a tendency to overlook or underestimate growing disintegrative forces in countries like Mexico, Colombia and Venezuela. At the same time, there remain significant "holdover" threats to the consolidation of democracy and regional stability. This essay will begin by discussing current U.S. national interests in the region, and assessing their relative importance to the United States. It will review today's regional security environment, and then go on to explore the most likely challenges to regional security and U.S. interests over the next two decades. Finally, it will evaluate how well U.S. strategy and military structures are equipped to pursue those interests, and make policy recommendations where appropriate.

The Importance of Latin America and the Caribbean to U.S. National Interests.

The U.S. National Security Strategy of "Engagement" is built on three core objectives: (1) Creating a stable, peaceful international security environment in which our nation, citizens and interests are not threatened; (2) Continuing American economic prosperity through increasingly open international trade and sustainable growth in the global economy; and (3) The promotion of democracy, human rights and the rule of law.[3]

At the same time, U.S. interests can be grouped into three categories: *Vital Interests*—that is, those of broad, overriding importance to the survival, safety and vitality of the nation; *Important Interests*—those which, while not affecting national survival, do affect our national well-being and the world in which we live; and *Peripheral Interests*—which might lead us to act because our values demand it, but which do not have a substantial impact on us.

How does Latin America fit into this scheme? The first thing that must be said is that in a hemisphere that is increasingly integrated and interdependent, the growth and prosperity of the Latin America economies will profoundly affect the prosperity of the United States. Latin America is the United States' fastest growing market, with exports in 1998 exceeding those going to the European Union.[4] By 2010, indeed, overall U.S. trade with the region is projected to exceed that with Europe and Japan combined. Some of this, at least, is of strategic importance.

Venezuela alone provides as much oil to the United States as do all of the Persian Gulf states together.[5] The continued provision of Venezuelan and Mexican petroleum, as well as access to the major new oil reserves of Colombia, constitutes an important—and arguably vital—U.S. interest which directly affects national well-being.

A second major interest is the promotion of democracy. At first glance, this might appear to be a peripheral concern. For much of its history, the United States was perfectly comfortable with authoritarian regimes in Latin America, so long as they did not threaten higher priority interests like regional security or U.S. economic holdings. But that is no longer the case. U.S. values have changed; democracy has been elevated to the status of an "important" interest. In part, this has been because American leaders have gained a greater appreciation of the role of legitimacy as a source of political stability. Governments that are popularly elected and respect human rights and the rule of law are less dangerous to both their citizens and their neighbors. Nations which are substantively democratic tend not to go to war with one another. They are also less vulnerable to the threat of internal war provoked, in part, by state violence and illegality and a lack of governmental legitimacy.[6]

In short, democracy and economic integration are not simply value preferences, but are increasingly bound up with hemispheric security. To take just one example: The restoration of democracy in Brazil and Argentina and their increasingly strong and profitable relationship in Mercosur have contributed in no small degree to their decisions to forsake the development of nuclear weapons. Perceptions of threat have declined, and perceptions of the benefits of cooperation have grown, and this has permitted progress on a range of security issues from border disputes, to peacekeeping, environmental protection, counternarcotics, and the combat of organized crime. Argentina has also developed a strong bilateral defense relationship with the United States, and is now considered a non-NATO ally.

This leads us to those interests which are most commonly defined as "vital"—i.e., the need to prevent or contain direct threats to the "survival, safety and vitality of our nation," including the "physical security of our territory and that of our allies, the safety of our citizens, our economic well-being and the protection of our critical infrastructure."[7] The most obvious threat of this kind would arise from the possession of Weapons of Mass Destruction by a hostile government or terrorist organization. The closest this hemisphere has come to such a scenario was during the Cuban Missile Crisis, though more recently there was concern about the spread of such weapons to the Southern Cone. That danger has been at least temporarily alleviated, however, with the result that the short- to medium- term threat from national governments is virtually nil. In military terms, the United States today is the undisputed hegemonic power in the hemisphere.

The situation with regard to subnational and transnational entities is considerably less sanguine. The principal security concerns in the hemisphere today are transnational in nature, stemming from such activities as drug trafficking, organized crime, money laundering, illegal immigration, and terrorism.[8] Of these, narcotrafficking probably poses the most serious danger. Illicit drugs account for roughly 14,000 U.S. deaths every year, and cost American society an estimated $110 billion.[9] The mafias have spread corruption and violence in numerous Latin American and Caribbean countries, subverting national institutions, endangering political stability, and making a mockery of the notion of sovereignty. The outlook for the future is not good.

Finally, the United States also has humanitarian and other concerns, including the need to respond to natural and manmade disasters, the preservation of human rights, demining, the promotion of sustainable development, and support for democratization and civilian control of the military.[10] While some of these interests may be peripheral, others are based on more than just ideological or humanitarian values. Some have security implications that might place them in a higher priority category. Human rights violations, for instance, did much to fuel the Central American conflicts of the 1970s and 1980s. And so did failed or corrupted attempts at disaster relief, such as the Nicaraguan government's response to the 1972 earthquake. In this sense, then, the international response to the recent devastation of Honduras and Nicaragua by Hurricane Mitch should be considered not simply a humanitarian effort, but an attempt to preserve political stability in a region that has only recently emerged from civil war.

The Current Latin America Security Environment: Threats and Challenges.

What are the major threats confronting Latin America, how do they affect U.S. security interests, and how is this configuration likely to change over the next quarter century? Currently, there are several concerns. One of the most important is the danger posed by economic instability. By late 1998, the international financial crisis that had begun in Asia in 1997, and then moved on to devastate Russia in the summer of 1998, hit Latin America. Brazil seemed to be teetering on the brink of disaster. Capital flight was depleting its reserves, raising questions about the country's ability to pay its short-term debt. As the eighth largest economy in the world, Brazil accounts for almost half of the output of Latin America, a region which buys roughly a fifth of U.S. exports. If the Brazilian economy went into a deep and prolonged recession, the spillover into other countries might trigger social and political turmoil that could endanger the region's young and still fragile democracies. Similarly, the impact on the U.S. banking system and economy would be substantial. More than 450 of the Fortune 500 companies do business in Brazil, which receives more direct foreign investment from the United States than any other country except China.[11] Fears about the country's economic health were already affecting the U.S. stock market.

With this in mind, in November 1998 the Clinton Administration and the International Monetary Fund announced a "precautionary" $41.5 billion aid package as part of a new strategy to help countries reform their economies before they were overwhelmed by the tumultuous global market forces sweeping the international system. Subsequently, President Fernando Henrique Cardoso persuaded a reluctant Congress to reduce social security benefits, a move foreign officials and investors viewed as a litmus test of the government's willingness to put the country's economic house in order. In January, the government announced it would allow the *real* to float on the global markets, resulting in a 40 percent plunge in its value. At that point, the country was rapidly moving into a recession, and the only question seemed to be how deep and prolonged it would be, and how much impact it would have on other Latin American countries.[12]

By June 1999, however, the situation had improved considerably. As early as April, Brazil made a triumphant return to the international capital markets. From near-record lows in the first turbulent days of the crisis, the stock market rose by over 50 percent, more than recovering its losses. Meanwhile, interest rates fell, and investment began flooding back into the country. Foreign reserves grew rapidly, inflation eased. While the central bank continued to buy and sell currency in the foreign exchange market to help stabilize the *real*, the objective now was no longer to prop it up but to prevent it from becoming too strong. Thus had "the sleepless nights of January" given way to a resurgence of optimism. Talk of a Brazilian "contagion" all but vanished. The only major downside was the continuing impact of the crisis on the Brazilian people, who still had to bear the burden of the austerity that had been imposed on them.[13]

What is striking about this episode is not just how quickly the crisis disappeared, but the continuing fragility and volatility of the Brazilian and Latin American economies. Clearly, economic analysts and investors had overestimated and overreacted to the initial signs of trouble. But just as clearly, they were also overly optimistic about the future. The bottom line is that the region's economies remain highly vulnerable to foreign shocks (e.g., low commodity prices for exports, financial crises half way around the world, a decision of the U.S. Federal Reserve to raise the discount rate), domestic mismanagement, and other destabilizing forces (the impact of hurricanes, earthquakes, etc.). Just how vulnerable was dramatized by a *Washington Post* headline in early August: "Deep Recession Envelops Latin America." By then, the region's economies (with the significant exceptions of Mexico and Peru) were being battered by a variety of forces, including low commodity prices, soaring public debt, high unemployment, currency destabilization, and a loss of foreign capital. In turn, this was inspiring a serious backlash against free market reforms, raising the prospect that the movement had reached its high-water mark and would now recede.[14]

A second major concern is the growing turmoil in the northwest quadrant of South America, especially in Colombia.[15] Until very recently the armed forces had been steadily losing ground to the estimated 20,000 Marxist guerrillas of the Colombian Revolutionary Armed Forces (FARC) and National Liberation Army (ELN). The rebels effectively control much of rural Colombia. Over the past several years, they have inflicted a number of significant military defeats on government forces. They are well-armed as a result of the war chest they have accumulated through drug taxes, kidnappings and a wide range of business investments.

Nor are these the only combatants. The most rapidly growing violent groups in the country today are right-wing paramilitary organizations which are waging a holy war against the guerrillas, sometimes in tacit alliance with local military commanders. There are now several thousand of these combatants. They are increasingly well-armed and organized, and are believed to be responsible for over 70 percent of the political killings in the country today. While the government is nowhere near collapse, the momentum until recently has been in favor of the guerrillas and paramilitaries. The danger is that Colombia will become increasingly balkanized and divided among regional warlords, and that the violence will spill over into neighboring countries. This process has already begun, especially in the Venezuelan and Panamanian borderlands, and it may be expected to get worse.

Closely related to these threats is the scourge of narcotrafficking. Violence and corruption have always been a problem in Colombia, as has the weakness of the state—its inability to command an effective presence—in rural areas. But the narco-revolution of the 1980s served as a catalyst for worsening these afflictions by channeling new resources (both financial and military) to old foes and creating new social actors, which transformed a polarized armed conflict between two sides (the armed forces and the guerrillas) into one in which multiple groups and sectors are armed.

The paramilitaries and guerrillas, of course, are not the only groups with ties to the narcos. The latter have penetrated all branches of government, from the national level to the local. While the case of Ernesto Samper (in which the former president accepted drug money for his presidential campaign) may be the most notorious instance, it should not obscure the fact that scores of congressmen have also accepted drug money in return for providing political protection for the mafias. Similarly, countless judges have let off narcos because of bribery or intimidation. Nor have military officers been exempt from such temptations. Or civil society, for that matter. The Colombian economy is far more dependent on narco-trafficking than is, for instance, the Mexican economy, and in the process of circulation these illicit funds taint virtually all social sectors. If anything, the country's current sharp economic downturn is likely to increase this dependency.[16]

In short, Colombia is an incipient narcostate. If the traffickers cannot control the political system, they have nevertheless had a profound influence. Even the destruction of the Medellin and Cali cartels has not diminished their empire, for in the aftermath the industry decentralized into smaller mafias which, in turn, have shifted much of the coca production from Peru and Bolivia to

Colombia. Today, Colombia has surpassed those countries to become the largest producer of raw coca in the world. Some 80 percent of the world's cocaine comes from within its borders. Needless to say, there has been no diminution of the flow of Colombian drugs (including marijuana and, increasingly, heroin) into the United States. All of which suggests that, while mafias and mafiosos may come and go, the basic problem remains unresolved. Nor is it likely to be resolved, at least not within the foreseeable future.

Venezuela also is entering perilous waters. It is increasingly unstable. The past couple of decades have witnessed severe socioeconomic decline and widespread corruption, which have decimated living standards[17] and undermined the legitimacy of the traditional political parties and the democratic system. The election in December 1998 of Lieutenant Colonel (retired) Hugo Chavez as president was a reflection of that discontent. Chavez is a populist messiah, whose allegiance to democracy is suspect. In 1992, he launched a bloody but unsuccessful *golpe de estado*. During his first year in office, he convened a Constituent Assembly, which has now rewritten the constitution, significantly expanding the powers of the Executive branch of government. The new charter abolishes the Senate, one of the two previously existing houses of Congress, and gives the president authority to dissolve the legislature under certain circumstances. The presidential term has been increased from 5 to 6 years, permitting Chavez to seek immediate reelection (which had been prohibited under the old constitution) and potentially allowing him to remain in office for another dozen years. The powers of states and municipalities have been reduced, as has civilian control over the armed forces. The state's role in managing the economy has been increased.[18]

The danger, of course, is that Chavez may use these new powers—which were overwhelmingly approved by popular vote in December 1999—to establish a dictatorship. What is occurring in Venezuela is a full-scale constitutional and institutional crisis pitting the Executive branch against the

Congress and Courts. The situation is increasingly polarized, with Chavez manipulating class resentments through demagogic appeals for social justice and a redistribution of national wealth. The issue is being framed as a choice between Good and Evil, with the president portraying himself as the supreme authority and personification of the people's will.[19] In the process, he has not hesitated to use threats and intimidation to get his way. He has militarized the government and society to an extent unwitnessed since the restoration of democracy in 1958. Numerous officers have been brought into the administration. Two hundred sixty-seven have been promoted, including 34 who were involved in his 1992 coup attempt, though there are not enough military posts for them to fill. At the same time, some 70,000 soldiers are being used in civic action projects, building schools, hospitals and roads, providing free medical care, selling food to the poor at below market prices. Soon, military doctrine will even be taught in the schools. Clearly, the armed forces are being courted. The president is trying to assure their loyalty and transform them into one of his power bases, while using them as an instrument for mobilizing mass support for the regime.

Where Chavez will go from here remains to be seen. His program is still largely at the stage of sweeping generalizations and bombastic appeals. It will have to be defined more concretely for fair judgments to be made. In addition to the constitutional changes mentioned above, the president has at various times suggested that he might stop payments on Venezuela's foreign debt and reverse key privatization initiatives in the petroleum industry. There are also some simmering resentments against the United States. Chavez has denied American counternarcotics planes permission to fly over Venezuelan territory, developed close relations with Fidel Castro, and is currently promoting a plan to construct a railroad track factory with China and Iran. The potential for angry rhetoric between Washington and Caracas is high, and Chavez might well succumb to the temptation—à la Fidel—of using the specter of a foreign enemy to mobilize domestic support should his economic and political problems prove intractable.

All this notwithstanding, some observers have raised questions about the quality of his radicalism. Chavez has not been above saying different things to different audiences. Moreover, as president he will have to operate within considerable constraints, not the least of which are the economic and political pressures the United States and the international community can bring on him to avoid radical economic measures and the breakdown of democracy. This being said, however, his election has alarmed not only Venezuela's traditional political and economic elites, but elites throughout the region. It has been a wake-up call that long-festering problems of poverty, inequality and corruption can no longer be ignored, lest the populace revolt and replace current leaders with a new generation of *caudillos* (strongmen), modeled perhaps along the lines of Chavez and his Peruvian counterpart, Alberto Fujimori, both of whom came to power through democratic means. At the same time, there is a fear, not simply of a return to the statist and protectionist policies of the past, but of the spread of the economic chaos and political instability they would probably engender.

How all this might affect the U.S. access to Venezuelan oil is not clear, but it is worth noting that we have a considerable stake in that pot. Venezuela is currently our leading foreign supplier of petroleum, and unstable Colombia next door ranks fifth. Whether a deterioration of U.S. relations with the Chavez government would endanger that access is difficult to say. This is not the 1960s, and Chavez does not have the option of turning to the Soviet Union as an alternative market and economic *patron* in the event of a breakdown of relations with the United States. Given the low international demand for oil in recent years, he might think twice about alienating his best customer. On the other hand, this past year has witnessed a spectacular increase in the price of petroleum. If that windfall continues, the constraints on the president would be eased considerably.

But as important as Brazil, Colombia, and Venezuela are to U.S. security interests, they pale beside Mexico. Few countries are more vital to the well-being of the United States than its neighbor to the south. Not only is Mexico our second largest trading partner, but the two countries share a 2,000-mile boundary. Any serious political or economic turmoil below the Rio Grande is almost certain to spill over the border in the form of illegal immigrants, political refugees, narcotrafficking, violence or corruption.

U.S. national security interests in Mexico are based on several concerns, the most important being (1) narcopolitics and drug trafficking, (2) political instability and violence, (3) insurgency, (4) economic crisis, and (5) the potential disruption of regional integration (in particular, the North American Free Trade Agreement [NAFTA]).

Of these threats, the first is the most pressing. The decade of the 1990s has witnessed an unprecedented growth and proliferation of major drug mafias. These syndicates have amassed huge fortunes, bought political protection at all levels of government, and engaged in internecine warfare against each other and anyone else unlucky enough to get in their way. In the process, they have so penetrated the Mexican state and socioeconomic structure that they have effectively subverted the country's institutions and undermined national sovereignty. You name the institution, and it has to one extent or another been corrupted: congress, the courts, state governors, the banks, businesses, the military, the police. The Federal Judicial Police have been so corrupted that it is no longer possible to make clear-cut distinctions between them and the criminals they are supposed to apprehend. In Mexico, the police very often are the crooks, and they have been deeply involved in narcotrafficking. Even the presidency has been touched, at least indirectly. There have been numerous reports of former cabinet members and other high officials with mafia connections. A former member of President Zedillo's and ex-President Salinas' security detail has admitted having been an operative for the Tijuana mafia. Salinas' brother,

Raul, probably had ties with the Gulf of Mexico cartel, and possibly with the Tijuana cartel as well.[20]

The ultimate danger, of course, is that Mexico might develop into a full-fledged narcostate. Already some 50-60 percent of the cocaine, up to 80 percent of the marijuana and 20-30 percent of the heroin imported into the United States comes from or through Mexico.[21] In addition, the Mexican mafias have dominated the methamphetamine "revolution" of the 1990s. These drugs are poisoning American society, destroying the social fabric, spreading crime and violence, and costing billions of dollars through lost productivity, medical expenses, incarceration of prisoners, and so on. The syndicates operate deep inside the United States, and there is mounting evidence of their corrupting effects on U.S. federal, state and local law enforcement agencies, financial institutions, and other socioeconomic and political structures. Even the U.S. military has been affected, as is evidenced by the several dozen servicemen investigated in recent years for drug running.[22] Should narcotics-related violence in Mexico escalate, moreover, the United States will not be immune. It will spread over the border. Indeed, it already has.[23]

Another danger, which seemed on the verge of realization during the traumatic year of 1994, is that Mexico might become "ungovernable."[24] This might occur in various forms and degrees, the worst case being a descent into anarchy or civil war. One possibility, for instance, might result from an intensification of the political struggles between the governing Party of Revolutionary Institutions (PRI) and the opposition Party of Democratic Revolution (PRD) and National Action Party (PAN). The PRI has lost a lot of ground in recent years. It no longer exercises the kind of dominance it did in the early 1990s, when Mario Vargas Llosa described Mexico as "the perfect dictatorship."[25] Today, it no longer controls the Mexico City government or the Chamber of Deputies. Many governorships are in the hands of the opposition. It is not at all unthinkable that an opposition candidate might win the presidency in the 2000 elections.[26] As the struggle for power intensifies, it could turn nasty.

The situation is also complicated by an internal power struggle within the PRI. While the modernizing technocratic elements have been able to capture the presidency during the last three national elections, imposing a reform agenda that has included NAFTA and a substantial transition towards democracy, the Old Guard party bosses or "dinosaurs" are attempting a comeback. They blame the *tecnicos* for the erosion of the PRI's political hegemony, and want to turn back the clock. The stakes are high, and the possibilities of violence cannot be dismissed, though, at this writing, party unity seems to have weathered the divisive November 1999 primary.[27] (Note: Some observers still believe that the 1994 assassinations of PRI presidential candidate Luis Donaldo Colosio and PRI secretary general Jose Francisco Ruiz Massieu were the product of such internal conflicts.)[28]

Even if Mexico is able to avoid major intra-elite and partisan violence, there remain serious doubts about the future. If the PRI loses power, what will replace it? The opposition is deeply divided between the leftist PRD and the rightist PAN. Can these very different tendencies cooperate with one another to effectively govern the country? One could conceive a situation, for instance, in which the PRD's Cuauhtemoc Cardenas wins the presidency, but then is stifled in his efforts to govern by a conservative PRI-PAN coalition. The ensuing political conflicts and immobilism could frighten foreign investors, damage the economy, and aggravate an already difficult socioeconomic situation.

Still another danger is the spread and intensification of the insurgencies that have cropped up in Chiapas and other (mostly southern) states during the past decade. The socioeconomic conditions that gave rise to these movements have not been eliminated, and in some respects have grown worse. Moreover, human rights violations by the military, local authorities, and paramilitary groups often linked to them have added to the volatility of the situation. While it is difficult to conceive of current conditions developing into the kind of massive revolutionary violence that swept the country early this century, things could certainly get worse. Another economic crisis would undoubtedly fuel the discontent. If at the same time Mexico experienced an upsurge of conflict from other sources (factional strife within the PRI, violence aimed at the political opposition, mafia-related killings, common crime) this combination of factors could potentially lead to a situation of ungovernability. Under such circumstances, the government might be tempted to return to more authoritarian methods to maintain order. Though unlikely, a military coup "to save the patria" is a possibility as is the rise of a civilian strongman, perhaps backed by the armed forces.

Beyond this, there is the uncertain course of the Mexican economy. For over two decades, the country has been on a rollercoaster ride of boom-bust cycles. In the process, hopes and expectations for a better future have been repeatedly raised, only to be dashed on the shoals of neoliberal reforms and unstable capital flows. There is no particular reason to think that the pattern will end soon. Though the Zedillo administration has done all the things the International Financial Institutions wanted, the growing interdependence of the world economic system means that economic shocks on the other side of the earth can have a traumatic effect on Latin America. Not until international mechanisms are created capable of preventing or at least minimizing such "contagion" will Mexico, or anyone else, be really secure. Along these same lines, there continues to be concern about how a slowdown of the U.S. economy and further moves by the Federal Reserve to raise the discount rate would affect Mexican economic growth and stability.

Nor can one be confident about the internal factors that can lead to crisis. Political instability and violence could still increase in the years ahead. Growing socioeconomic inequalities and poverty, worsened by neoliberal reforms, could trigger popular unrest. New governments could come into office less committed to marketization and privatization, or even pledging to turn back reforms already made.

Such developments could spark capital flight and thrust the economy into a downward spiral. One indicator to watch is how the economy behaves as the 2000 elections approach. Ever since the mid-1970s, Mexico has suffered from a syndrome in which the economy has been subjected to disruption or decline as each administration has drawn to a close. Will Zedillo be able to escape the "curse of the Mexican presidents"? Will his successors?

Finally, all this has implications for the future of U.S. economic relations both with Mexico and the rest of the hemisphere. Political and economic turmoil could give ammunition to opponents of the North American Free Trade Agreement, both in the United States and Mexico. This would be especially likely if the narcotrafficking situation worsened and high-level Mexican officials (for instance, the president) were implicated. The ensuing uproar would certainly trigger demands for decertification in the U.S. Senate, which in turn would lead to a nationalistic reaction in Mexico. In the midst of all this, protectionists on both sides would no doubt demand that NAFTA's pull-out clause be activated. If successful, such a move would have a devastating impact on U.S. economic and political interests in Mexico, and would toll the death knell for any hope of expanding NAFTA into a hemisphere-wide Free Trade Area of the Americas.

Pitfalls and Prospects of the Future.

And what of U.S. national security interests and objectives in the hemisphere 20 years from now? In general, they will be pretty much what they are today. The United States will seek to shape a stable, peaceful regional security environment; it will try to foster American prosperity through expanding trade and regional economic growth; and it will in all likelihood continue to promote democracy, human rights and the rule of law. Thus, many of the challenges we will face will reflect current problems.

One of the most obvious needs between then and now will be the creation of mechanisms to maintain the stability of the emerging new international economic system. As Jose Antonio Ocampo has noted, the world faces a systemic crisis associated with the "enormous asymmetry existing between an increasingly sophisticated and dynamic international financial world and the absence of a suitable institutional framework to regulate this." While in the short run the answer is expansionist policies in the industrial economies, there is a long-term need for far-reaching reform of the international financial establishment, increasing Latin America's capacity to handle financial volatility with its own fiscal, financial and exchange instruments.[29] If this is not done, the consequence is likely to be chronic economic instability. Economic crises would become more frequent, along with the social and political turmoil they engender. The implications for personal security, political stability and democracy would not be salutary.[30]

But even if international economic stability can be established, one cannot be confident about the prospects for political stability. The neoliberal model of economic development has not yet proven it can generate an equitable distribution of wealth. Thus far, indeed, it has had a polarizing impact, increasing the gaps between rich and poor. Whether this is a short-term phenomenon, which will be reversed once economic stability is attained and the benefits of growth "trickle down" to the masses, or whether the inequalities and poverty generated will prove intractable cannot be predicted with confidence. Should the latter be the case, however, it will make the task of maintaining political legitimacy and stability that much more difficult. As Cynthia McClintock has noted, formal democracy is not enough.[31] Unless people believe that a political system provides tangible benefits—e.g., improved living conditions, law and order, respect for human rights—they may withhold their support or cast it to demagogues or guerrilla groups who promise "real" democracy or a more fully "developed" democracy, or who reject liberal democracy altogether in favor of *caudillo* rule, anocracy, or "totalitarian democracy."[32]

And let there be no mistake, there will be an abundance of societal and political weaknesses for such leaders to exploit. Unless rural areas can be rejuvenated and made economically viable for their inhabitants, problems of landlessness and land poverty will continue to provide the raw materials for insurgency and urban migration. At the same time, continuing rapid urban population growth, with all the attendant problems of decapitalization, corruption, unemployment, violent crime, and poverty, will create conditions fostering "ungovernability," including terrorism, insurgency, and an enhanced role for the military in internal security. The upshot will be continuing large-scale migration to the United States, which will serve as an escape valve to avoid social explosion, and quite possibly a return to less democratic forms of governance.

One must place this within the context of the region's history. In the past, Latin American countries have gone through cycles of democracy and dictatorship. While a wholesale authoritarian restoration could conceivably occur again, a more plausible scenario would be a limited reversion, with the pendulum swinging only partway back. Thus, most countries would remain more-or-less democratic, with some developing more substantive democracy, others combining democratic form with authoritarian substance, and a few perhaps reverting to outright dictatorship. Needless to say, authoritarian restorations would be most likely where democratically elected governments lose legitimacy because of a failure to meet popular expectations.[33]

Where are the greatest danger points? Certainly, the three countries discussed earlier—Colombia, Venezuela, and Mexico—will all bear close watching. At present, the Colombian crisis continues to worsen, with no end in sight. One should remember that this is a nation which has been torn by violence for half a century. It is by no means unthinkable that it may still be in turmoil 20 years from now. The exact form may change, as it has in the past. It might assume the shape of *de facto* balkanization—the division of the country into more-or-less distinct territories ruled by different authorities (e.g., government, guerrilla, paramilitary). Or there might be interminable civil strife, left-wing or right-wing dictatorship, or even the development of a full-fledged narcostate. It is also possible that Colombia's contagion might spread to its neighbors, infecting them with the kind of violence and narcoactivity commonly subsumed under the rubric of "Colombianization."

The outlook for Venezuela is not quite as bleak. Nevertheless, the current crisis has been incubating for several decades, and during the past 10 years it has gotten much worse. At this point, there is no way of confidently forecasting the country's political future. Democracy may ultimately survive, but in the short run at least the country seems to be heading into a period of *caudillo* rule, which may or may not be cloaked in a democratic facade. Venezuela is blessed with an abundance of natural resources—most notably petroleum—so its economic condition should eventually improve, assuming oil prices stabilize at reasonably high levels, the government doesn't frighten away investors or otherwise mismanage the economy, and some semblance of regional economic stability can be achieved. But whether the distribution of national wealth will become any more equitable is problematic. The bottom line is that the Venezuelan crisis is not likely to end any time soon and could conceivably drag on for a decade or more.

Of the three countries discussed earlier, Mexico probably has the best chance of passing through its "time of troubles" relatively unscathed. Even so, the future remains fraught with hazards. Its nascent democracy may continue to develop and deepen, or it may stagnate or even regress. And even if the country experiences considerable economic development—as it almost certainly will—that growth will probably be uneven, with boom-bust cycles and a maldistribution of wealth continuing to undermine political stability and democratization. For the United States, the greatest challenges will probably be: (1) the continuation of the narcothreat from Mexican mafias, allied with Colombian and other foreign drug syndicates; and (2) illegal immigration. There will be a growing temptation to use the U.S. military to deal with these challenges.

Arguably, the primary security threat in the hemisphere today is narcotrafficking.[34] It is a problem that is not likely to go away. According to the 1998 *Strategic Assessment* of National Defense University's Institute for National Strategic Studies:

> The illegal drug market long ago achieved stability and, in some cases, saturation, and that situation is unlikely to change any time soon. Without a major change in counterdrug policy and methodology, the only measurable change in the market will be in methods of smuggling or in market taste.[35]

While it is difficult to take seriously the kind of disaster scenario posited by former Secretary of Defense Caspar Weinberger, in which the United States and Mexico actually go to war over the issue,[36] one can certainly imagine the use of Special Operations Forces to, for instance, drop down in Ciudad Juarez or Tijuana to capture some local drug kingpin. Such actions would probably be unilateral in nature, the by-product of growing U.S. frustration with Mexican authorities' unwillingness or inability to stem the narcotics trade, and would severely aggravate already strained relations between the two countries. Again, the implications for NAFTA and, by extension, regional economic integration could be considerable.

Another possible scenario might involve a growing U.S. military presence and aid program, designed to combat the mafias and/or guerrilla groups. Here Colombia, rather than Mexico,[37] may become the primary troublespot. U.S. counternarcotics aid to that country is rapidly increasing. (Counterdrug aid in 1999 is $289 million, more than three times the level in 1998, and a tenfold increase over a 5-year period. Colombia now receives more U.S. aid than any other country except Israel and Egypt. This assistance, moreover, is likely to increase substantially over the next several years.)[38] Currently, there are at least 100-150 American military personnel in the country at any given time, training Colombian soldiers, manning radar sites, gathering intelligence and performing other functions.[39]

For the moment, at least, the United States is trying to maintain a distinction between counternarcotics and counterinsurgency, with aid being given solely for the former. But whether this selectivity can be maintained indefinitely is anybody's guess. If the situation on the battlefield worsens, the United States may, like it or not, become increasingly involved in a counterinsurgency war. In any case, the distinction between insurgency and narcotrafficking is not clear-cut; in Colombia the two phenomena are interrelated. Much of the counterdrug assistance is fungible; moreover, operations can easily cross the line. Crop eradication efforts, for instance, are usually not directed against traffickers, but against peasant cultivators of coca, amapola and marijuana. Unfortunately, by attacking *campesino* growers, counternarcotics operations risk pushing them into the arms of the guerrillas and paramilitaries, thus increasing the violence and the threat to the Colombian state. Similarly, targeting the areas of illegal crop cultivation and transit may simply push these activities into other territories or countries. This has been an all too common pattern in the past. The upshot has been the spread, rather than the eradication, of the affliction.

Three other countries where the United States may very well become militarily involved are Cuba, Haiti, and Panama. The transition to a post-Castro era has already begun. The only questions are how long it will take, whether it can be achieved peacefully, whether the political system that emerges will be democratic, and whether some kind of foreign military presence will accompany the transition.

With regard to the first question, it is likely that we are still some years away from the post-Castro era. The Castro brothers clearly intend to stay the course, with Raul designated as Fidel's successor in the event the older brother dies first. While the Castros could go at any time (both have had health problems in recent years), they could also very well linger on indefinitely. Fidel, it should be remembered, is only 73 years old.[40] So no one should be surprised if the year 2010 dawns with at least one of the brothers still in power.

The more interesting questions involve how the transition will develop once the Castros depart. Raul is widely held to be a temporary figure. Lacking Fidel's charisma and authority, he nevertheless commands considerable support because of his name, history, and positions as Second Secretary of the Cuban Communist Party and Minister of Defense. Whether he or Fidel will designate a post-Castro successor, or try to create a constitutional or institutional mechanism for choosing one, remains to be seen. In any event, there will probably be a succession struggle. Whether it turns violent or not cannot be predicted. If it does, however, there will undoubtedly be calls for a military intervention from influential Cuban-American groups and their allies in Congress. Here, massive refugee flows may also create strong pressures and temptations to intervene. If such a course were chosen, it could result in substantial resistance and bloodshed, requiring a prolonged military occupation, perhaps souring U.S.-Cuban relations for decades more.

Another scenario involves the possibility of a regime disintegration while Fidel is still in power. Some analysts have raised the specter of a *Götterdammerung*. According to this line of thought, if Castro were in danger of being ousted by an internal revolt he might prefer to go out with a bang rather than a whimper. He has always craved historical greatness. What better way to assure it, at this late stage in his career, than by launching an air assault on the U.S. nuclear power plant at Turkey Point, in South Florida? Or—in a variation of that scenario—biological weapons might be used in an attack.[41]

This scenario is plausible enough so that U.S. defense planners must take it into account. But it is not very likely to occur. For one thing, Castro has created an extraordinary system of controls, which will probably prevent successful revolutions from "above" (i.e., through a *golpe de estado*) or "below" (via a mass uprising) for as long as he is alive and functioning.[42] Moreover, for all his sins, one may doubt whether he really wants to go down in history as a mass murderer. If the United States were poised to invade or attack Cuba, however, that would be another matter, and U.S. policymakers should keep that in mind. During the Cuban Missile Crisis, it will be recalled, Castro urged Khrushchev to launch a nuclear strike against the United States if the latter invaded the island.[43]

But even if Castro, under desperate circumstances, were to resort to desperate measures, it is by no means clear that he would be able to successfully carry out a strike against a target like Turkey Point. As Albert Coll has pointed out, it is one thing for Cuban jets to stealthily approach U.S. territory in peacetime, as has happened in the past, but quite another in time of crisis, when American air defense systems would presumably be in a state of heightened alert. And as for the biological warfare scenario, even if he has biological agents available (and some observers believe he does), it is unclear how much progress has been made in adapting them for use as weapons.[44]

A more likely possibility is that in the midst of a crisis Castro might open up the floodgates of emigration and use his "boat people" card to defuse pent-up tension and divert popular outrage away from his regime onto fleeing refugees, the United States, and the Miami exile community. He has done this before, most tellingly in 1980 and 1994, and it could happen again. The United States must be prepared for such an eventuality.

Finally, there has been an ongoing concern in U.S. political circles about the possibility of a nuclear accident at the unfinished Russian technology nuclear plant at Juragua. Indeed, the Defense Department has authorized the creation of a Caribbean Radiation Early Warning System (CREWS) to monitor possible leaks from the facility. More recently, however, Castro announced the indefinite suspension of the Juragua project due to a lack of financing, effectively defusing the issue. Nevertheless, given the island's continuing energy needs, one should not be surprised if the nuclear option is raised again at some point.[45]

Haiti, too, is a potential candidate for intervention. The country was the object of the most recent U.S. military invasion, in September 1994, when more than 20,000 troops were sent in to depose a brutal military dictatorship and restore the government of President Jean-Bertrand Aristide. Yet, all the king's horses and all the king's men have not been able to put the country together again. Haiti remains a "failed state"—a society torn by the inability of its political leaders to cooperate with one another, propped up by foreign doles and the unspoken but acutely felt prospect of another intervention should things once again fall apart. While there has been progress in some areas—most notably, in the formation of a Haitian National Police—given the country's long cyclical history of despotism and anarchy, and the continuing domestic political strife it is experiencing,[46] it seems likely that sooner or later its democratic experiment will collapse, violence and refugee flows will ensue, and some foreign military presence may again be needed to maintain order and civility.[47]

Another potential trouble spot—though somewhat less so than Cuba and Haiti—is Panama. The strategic value of the Panama Canal is no longer much of an issue.[48] The Cold War is over, the Soviet and Cuban threats no longer exist, and the U.S. military presence has now been terminated. Still, the waterway remains "one of the world's crucial 'choke-points' for oceanborne traffic, controlling a significant portion of international commerce."[49] The United States continues to have an important interest in the canal's physical protection, and arguably has the right to intervene militarily to reopen it or restore its operations in the event that it is closed or no longer functioning.[50]

Under what circumstances might such an intervention occur? One issue, certainly, is the possibility of a hostile foreign involvement. (Opponents of the canal turnover have recently designated China as the prime candidate for this role.) Another concern is Panamanian political stability. For most of this century, a strong American military presence has served as a deterrent to foreign threats and, more debatably, Panamanian domestic turmoil.[51] Now that deterrent—always as much psychological as physical—has been removed. Will Panama perhaps fall prey to instability and dictatorship? Such things have happened in the past. Currently, moreover, the country must deal with increasing incursions from Colombian narcotraffickers, guerrillas and paramilitaries. Might not these developments, if they continue to worsen, eviscerate the nation's sovereignty? Might not Panama, for instance, become a narcostate? The fact that it has only a constabulary rather than a standing military raises questions about its ability to withstand such threats. Moreover, beyond this, Panamanian politicians may not be able to resist the temptation of treating the canal as a *piñata*—a fabulous opportunity for graft—in the process neglecting its upkeep and modernization and endangering its future utility. What would the United States do under those circumstances?

Some of these dangers are more credible than others. The China scenario, in particular, seems a bit far-fetched. The "threat" in question is based largely on the award of port concessions at both ends of the canal to Hutchison Whampoa, a Hong Kong firm. According to some U.S. conservatives, the company will be a puppet of the Chinese military and could block American ships from entering the waterway. But this ignores the fact that the ports have no control over the entry to the canal and that Chinese attempts to interfere with U.S. access would violate the facility's neutrality and almost certainly trigger an American military response. China would find itself in a similar position to the Soviet Union during the Cuban Missile Crisis—eyeball-to-eyeball with the United States in a region of overwhelming U.S. strength and equally overwhelming Chinese weakness. Nor can the Chinese military threat be compared to the Soviet threat in 1962.

China is still a poor country, with very limited military capabilities far from its borders.

Moreover, even if some of these problems did materialize, they would not necessarily constitute direct threats. Panamanian political instability, for instance, might have little effect on the canal's operations. Nevertheless, the U.S. Southern Command is sufficiently concerned that it is conducting contingency planning for an intervention, "cooperatively with the Panamanians, or unilaterally if the condition dictates."[52]

While we are in a speculative mode, it may be useful to raise the issue of whether, two or three decades from now, the United States might have to deal with a regional hegemon or peer competitor. The most obvious candidate for such a role would be Brazil, which already accounts for almost half of Latin America's economic production and has by far the largest armed forces in the region (313,250 active troops).[53] That country could very well assume a more commanding political and military role in the decades ahead.

Until recently, the primary U.S. concern about Brazil has been that it might acquire nuclear weapons and delivery systems. In the 1970s, the Brazilian military embarked on a secret program to develop an atom bomb. By the late 1980s, both Brazil and Argentina were aggressively pursuing nuclear development programs that had clear military spin-offs.[54] There were powerful military and civilian advocates of developing nuclear weapons and ballistic missiles within both countries. Today, however, the situation has changed. As a result of political leadership transitions in both countries, Brazil and Argentina now appear firmly committed to restricting their nuclear programs to peaceful purposes. They have entered into various nuclear-related agreements with each other—most notably the quadripartite comprehensive safeguards agreement (1991), which permits the inspection of all their nuclear installations by the International Atomic Energy

Agency—and have joined the Missile Technology Control Regime.

Even so, no one can be certain about the future. As Scott Tollefson has observed:

> . . . the military application of Brazil's nuclear and space programs depends less on technological considerations than on political will. While technological constraints present a formidable barrier to achieving nuclear bombs and ballistic missiles, that barrier is not insurmountable. The critical element, therefore, in determining the applications of Brazil's nuclear and space technologies will be primarily political.[55]

Put simply, if changes in political leadership were instrumental in redirecting Brazil's nuclear program towards peaceful purposes, future political upheavals could still produce a reversion to previous orientations. Civilian supremacy is not so strong that it could not be swept away by a coup, especially if the legitimacy of the current democratic experiment were to be undermined by economic crisis and growing poverty/inequality. Nor are civilian leaders necessarily less militaristic or more committed to democracy than the military. The example of Peru's Fujimori comes immediately to mind.

How serious a threat might Brazil potentially be? It has been estimated that if the nuclear plant at Angra dos Reis (Angra I) were only producing at 30 percent capacity, it could produce five 20-kiloton weapons a year. If production from other plants were included, Brazil would have a capability three times greater than India or Pakistan. Furthermore, its defense industry already has a substantial missile producing capability. On the other hand, the country has a very limited capacity to project its military power via air and sealift or to sustain its forces over long distances. And though a 1983 law authorizes significant military manpower increases (which could place Brazil at a numerical level slightly higher than France, Iran and Pakistan), such growth will be restricted by a lack of economic resources. Indeed, the development of all these military potentials has been, and will continue to be, severely constrained by a lack of money. (Which is one reason Brazil decided to engage in arms control with Argentina in the first place.)[56]

In short, a restoration of Brazilian militarism, imbued with nationalistic ambitions for great power status, is not unthinkable, and such a regime could present some fairly serious problems. That government would probably need foreign as well as domestic enemies to help justify its existence. One obvious candidate would be the United States, which would presumably be critical of any return to dictatorial rule. Beyond this, moreover, the spectre of a predatory international community, covetous of the riches of the Amazon, could help rally political support to the regime. For years, some Brazilian military officers have been warning of "foreign intervention." Indeed, as far back as 1991 General Antenor de Santa Cruz Abreu, then chief of the Military Command of the Amazon, threatened to transform the region into a "new Vietnam" if developed countries tried to "internationalize" the Amazon. Subsequently, in 1993, U.S.-Guyanese combined military exercises near the Brazilian border provoked an angry response from many high-ranking Brazilian officers.[57]

Since then, of course, U.S.-Brazilian relations have improved considerably. Nevertheless, the basic U.S./international concerns over the Amazon—the threat to the region's ecology through burning and deforestation, the presence of narcotrafficking activities, the Indian question, etc.—have not disappeared, and some may very well intensify in the years ahead. At the same time, if the growing trend towards subregional economic groupings—in particular, MERCOSUR—continues, it is likely to increase competition between Southern Cone and NAFTA countries. Economic conflicts, in turn, may be expected to intensify political differences, and could lead to heightened politico-military rivalry between different blocs or coalitions in the hemisphere.

Even so, there continue to be traditional rivalries and conflicts within MERCOSUR, especially between Brazil and its neighbors, and these will certainly complicate the group's evolution. Among other things, the past year witnessed a serious deterioration of relations between Brazil and Argentina, the product partly of the former's January 1999 currency devaluation, which severely strained economic ties between the two countries. In part, too, these conflicts were aggravated by Argentina's (unsuccessful) bid to join the North Atlantic Treaty Organization (NATO), which Brazilians interpreted as an attempt to gain strategic advantage. The upshot was that relations soured to the extent where questions have been raised as to the continued viability of MERCOSUR itself. In light of these problems, one cannot but wonder what impact a resurgence of Brazilian authoritarianism, combined with a push for regional hegemonic status, would have on Argentina, currently a "non-NATO ally" of the United States.

Finally, closer to home, there is the difficult problem of U.S. border defense. One suspects that the years ahead will witness growing pressure to use Department of Defense personnel and resources to bolster law enforcement agencies patrolling U.S. frontiers to prevent illegal immigration and drug smuggling. (Indeed, legislation has already been proposed authorizing the deployment of up to 10,000 more troops on the Southwest Border. In late 1998, however, the bill was rejected by the Senate.) Since 1990, the military has been engaged in several thousand operations along the frontier, running listening posts to assist the Border Patrol in tracking drugs and migrants, building fences and barriers, repairing roads, and helping law enforcement agencies in counternarcotics operations. Yet, notwithstanding this aid, civilian agencies continue to be stretched thin. The amount of drugs coming over the border has not been significantly reduced, and law enforcement officials often find themselves outgunned and outmanned by their adversaries. Consequently, there is an increasing temptation to look to the military for answers.[58]

Conclusions and Caveats.

The preceding analysis, it must be emphasized, is more in the realm of speculation about *potential* problems than a prediction. Latin America is a huge and enormously complex region, and the farther into the future one attempts to extrapolate from current trends and realities, the less accurate the forecast is likely to be. Yet, even if one takes a more optimistic view of the future than I am inclined to do,[59] the previous pages should provide ample warning against complaisance. The next quarter century is as likely to be marked by political turmoil, violence, poverty and inequality as by democratization and socioeconomic development.

It is especially important that this be recognized because U.S. attention to Latin America has historically ebbed and flowed. Unless there is a crisis, we tend to take the region for granted. Economic ties may be an exception, but even here our attitude is ambivalent, as witnessed by Congress' unwillingness to grant the Clinton administration "fast-track" authority for an extension of NAFTA to Chile. Benign neglect is our preferred posture. As Scotty Reston once observed, Americans will do anything for Latin Americans except read about them.

The problem is that what happens in Latin America matters. Regional stability deeply affects U.S. national interests and security, and unless the United States remains engaged it is likely to find itself unprepared for crises when they arise. And they *will* arise. If we have learned anything from history, it is that bad times always return. In the past, this has often led to overreaction and ill-advised interventions, which we are still paying for today in the form of the distrust they have sown among our southern neighbors. One consequence is that the United States has no real military alliances in the Latin American theater.[60]

Thus, it is difficult to argue with President Clinton's "imperative of engagement" or the National Military

Strategy's admonition that we must "Shape, Respond, and Prepare Now."[61] In theory at least, if we are successful in shaping the environment there will be no need for a military response because we will have forestalled or deterred any threats that might arise.[62]

The problem is that there are severe limitations on the ability of the United States to perform the shaping function. In the words of one U.S. Southern Command (SOUTHCOM) observer: "We do a pretty good job of reacting and preparing," but "shaping is more problematic."[63]

This is so for a number of reasons. One is the sheer magnitude of the task and the inability of U.S. influence to compete with Latin American domestic influences in affecting the course of political, economic, social and military development in these countries. Thus, even the frequently cited "success" of the Reagan administration in promoting democracy was due less to U.S. efforts than those of Latin Americans. U.S. influence may have been decisive in a handful of countries—El Salvador, Honduras and Grenada come to mind—but elsewhere internal forces held sway.[64] More recently, while U.S. military power was able to oust dictatorships in Panama (1989) and Haiti (1994), the subsequent democratization of those countries depended at least as much on Panamanians and Haitians as on the United States. (Is Haiti really a democracy? In form perhaps, but not in much else.)

In short, except on those rare occasions where power is exercized overwhelmingly, as in an invasion or the supply of massive aid to a dependent client state, the United States will have to rely on more subtle and less effective means to shape the environment. Influence rather than power will be the name of the game.

Beyond this, the U.S. ability to influence will be sharply limited by a severe lack of resources. Foreign aid has dried up in the post-Cold War era. Even SOUTHCOM is stretched thin. The byword there is that: "We are an economy of force theater, but it is not free. It doesn't take much, but it does take something."[65]

Now, SOUTHCOM is not really a warfighting command. Rather, shaping and engagement are its primary activities. It has very few troops, especially in comparison to the much larger and better resourced CINCdoms like the European Command (EUCOM). Thus, if soldiers are needed for an invasion, they will have to be obtained from a "force provider" such as the U.S. Joint Forces Command (previously known as the Atlantic Command).[66] While over 48,000 troops rotated through Central and South America in 1998, fully 35 percent came from the Reserve and National Guard. This included special operations forces, humanitarian, peacekeeping and road-building brigades, counterdrug trainers, and personnel sent to relieve active duty troops and provide operational support.[67] Significantly, the recent shift from bilateral to multilateral exercises in this AOR has been driven by a lack of resources.

Another problem is that the United States often cannot predict the consequences of its own actions. Second and third order effects are difficult to calculate. Even with the best of intentions (and U.S. intentions are not always pure), American policy sometimes has precisely the opposite effect of what is intended. Indeed, J. Patrice McSherry, in an important article on "The Emergence of 'Guardian Democracy,'" argues that there is a central contradiction in the Clinton administration's Latin American strategy: While encouraging democracy, on the one hand, the United States is simultaneously strengthening the very forces (the military) that have traditionally constituted the greatest threat to democracy in the region. The upshot has been the containment and weakening of democratic institutions and processes, and the development of a hybrid form of authoritarian democracy.

At the heart of the argument is the contention that the economic hardships and social dislocations caused by U.S. economic strategy (neoliberalism) have led many Latin American governments to adopt authoritarian measures in order to maintain public order/national security. Thus, civilian presidents, allied with military forces, are creating truncated and militarized forms of democracy as they simultaneously carry out economic restructuring, often by decree. . . . Executives have used national security laws reminiscent of the military states and mobilized the military and security forces to enforce order.

In turn, new U.S.-sponsored roles and missions for the armed forces have drawn them deeper into the political realm and legitimized their involvement in social control and guardianship activities.[68]

McSherry argues that six trends epitomize the danger in countries as diverse as Peru, Argentina, Mexico, Chile, Colombia, Brazil, and Bolivia: (1) the enlargement of the military presence in civilian institutions; (2) the use of authoritarian practices by civilian governments; (3) new internal security and domestic-intelligence doctrines and missions for the military; (4) the use of political intelligence organizations; (5) continued impunity for violators of human rights; and, (6) acts by paramilitary groups and unregulated private security organizations. To this might perhaps be added a seventh trend, namely the recent tendency for retired military officers to enter presidential politics (as in the successful election campaigns of Presidents Banzer in Bolivia and Chavez in Venezuela, and the less successful efforts of Lino Oviedo in Paraguay and Harold Bedoya in Colombia).

These are important developments, and they underscore the hazards of not coming to terms with the basic socioeconomic challenges mentioned earlier—most notably, poverty, inequality, and the problem of economic instability/volatility. They should also caution against an uncritical embrace of military-to-military cooperation. At minimum, they suggest that strengthening the military without a corresponding strengthening of civilian institutions and leadership can gut democracy of much of its substance. Clearly, there is a critical need to bolster civilian control of the military, as well as civilian competence in national security affairs. Just as evident, there is an ongoing need to cultivate understanding of and respect for democracy among both militaries and civilians. The problem of authoritarianism is not restricted to the former. The recent examples of Fujimori in Peru and Menem in Argentina, in particular, demonstrate that civilians too can be *caudillos*. Intimidation of the political opposition, harassment of the press, human rights abuses, and *continuismo* can be just as much a part of civilian rule as military rule.

It is in part within this context that one must place the expanding roles and missions issue. The concern, of course, is that the increasing involvement of the armed forces in "new" missions such as counternarcotics, law enforcement, counterterrorism and infrastructural development will militarize society and politics to an unhealthy extent, undermining civilian institutions and leadership, increasing human rights violations, and severely constraining the further development of these nascent and still very fragile democracies.[69] The dangers are very real, especially in countries where the professionalization of the military has been only partial or incomplete. There the assumption of new roles and missions could lead to the politicization of the military in a pattern reminiscent of the 1960s experiences with nationbuilding and "civic action."

Yet, it is crucial that the total context be considered. If the dangers of "militarization" are real, so are the dangers of not coming to terms with new threats to national security. If civilian institutions are incapable of dealing with the rise of drug cartels and rapidly escalating criminal violence, for instance, governments may feel they have little choice than to call on the armed forces. In such situations, the risks and costs of inaction—whether it be the corruption and weakening of political institutions, the loss of national sovereignty to substate actors (e.g., mafias), or other dangers—may be prohibitive.

The bottom line is that the United States must remain engaged. We have an important role to play in fostering regional peace, security, democratic values, and a respect for human rights. To take just two recent examples: In the summer of 1998, U.S. military-to-military contacts with members of the Peruvian and Ecuadoran Armed Forces helped defuse tensions and encourage a separation of forces at a time when unrest threatened to ignite armed conflict and derail the peaceful resolution of that border dispute. About the same time, senior members of the Southern Command personally intervened with Paraguayan military leaders when it appeared that extraconstitutional measures might be invoked during that country's electoral crisis. In both of these cases, engagement activities and the development of personal relationships between U.S. and Latin American military leaders created opportunities for constructive dialogue and mediation that might not otherwise have been available. Similarly, the Southern Command has made a considerable effort to incorporate human rights instruction into its training programs for Latin American militaries. And there is reason to believe that this has had some effect.[70]

In short, U.S. isolationism would be counterproductive. It would send precisely the wrong message—namely, that we don't care. Such signals would not improve civil liberties or dissuade the military from intervening in political affairs. Rather, they would pave the way for the reemergence or revitalization of some of the worst aspects of the traditional political culture. Authoritarianism and submission have deep roots in the Latin American psyche. One of the dangers in the current situation is that the military may be simply undergoing a kind of institutional hypothermia or "cocooning," temporarily retrenching and adopting a low profile to protect its corporate interests while awaiting a more favorable future climate in which to reassert itself. U.S. leaders should be alert to such potential developments, and should discourage them where feasible. At the same time, Latin American countries face very real security threats, which cannot be ignored lest they lead to even more dangerous situations. The United States must help them meet these needs.

Recommendations.

Military-to-military engagement will be an important part of the emerging U.S. strategy towards Latin America in the 21st century. But it is not an end in itself. It is a means of pursuing a much broader range of objectives, including regional stability and security, democracy, human rights, and socioeconomic development. The overall strategy must be coherent and comprehensive, and it must clearly define and relate ends, ways and means. (What, exactly, are the objectives of the strategy? What resources are necessary to attain them? How—in what ways—can those means be employed to achieve the goals being sought?) The strategy must be devised primarily by civilian leaders, though clearly in consultation with the military. Once defined, both civilian and military leaders must exercise the necessary oversight to make sure that policy implementation is done in a way that does not inadvertently subvert the primary aims of the strategy. Put simply, strategy must drive operations, rather than vice versa. Without proper supervision, there is always a danger that those who implement policy will actually make policy.

This has sometimes been a problem in both civilian and military bureaucracies. A narrow focus on building military-to-military contacts, for instance, can obscure the forest for the trees. In the words of one human rights observer: "The United States runs the risk of having [SOUTHCOM] set its own policy."[71] It is easy to forget that the recipients of military aid have interests and agendas of their own, which are often different from the interests of either Latin American civilians or the United States. At minimum, greater attention should be paid to strengthening civilian institutions and leadership. In many Latin American countries, the armed forces still exercise disproportionate political power. Too often, civilians have been reluctant to exert their authority in areas where the military has traditionally been dominant. In this, they may have been too timid.[72]

Thus, my first recommendation is that the United States do more to redress the historical imbalance in Latin American civil-military relations by seeking to strengthen civilian institutions, both in the state and civil society. Police and judicial reform should be a priority. As matters now stand, many governments feel they have no choice but to bring the armed forces into law enforcement. The alternative is rampant criminality and national insecurity. Only when civilian law enforcement institutions are strengthened—professionalized, purged of incompetent, corrupt and brutal elements, and given more resources—will they be able to perform the missions they were designed for. A failure on this score would mean that militarization would become a semi-permanent feature of the emerging Latin American political order—or at least a chronic resort wherever civilian institutions fail.

U.S. policy with respect to police training is especially in need of review. Currently, it is largely paralyzed by Section 660a of the Foreign Assistance Act. There is here no small irony. As Ambassador (retired) David Passage has pointed out, we have no problem with training Latin American militaries in law enforcement—though we would never allow our own armed forces to police the United States—but we refuse to train civilian police.[73] Such restrictions do nothing to professionalize or improve the human rights performance of the police; they merely weaken civilian control of the military. It is past time to lift them.

Greater efforts must also be made in the vetting and training of judicial personnel. It will do little good to try to improve the quality of police forces if judges—whether through incompetence, bribery or intimidation—simply turn loose the guilty. Such behavior only undermines morale and fosters cynicism and human rights abuse, as officers resort to extra-judicial justice to punish those whom the courts do not.

Nor are these the only challenges. Most Latin American countries have achieved formal democracy. The next step is to go beyond the forms to more substantive democracy.

Among other things, this will require political leadership training, civic education, corruption control, and the fostering of strong political parties and civil societies. How all this can be done in an era of declining U.S. will to provide foreign aid is not immediately apparent. But the consequences of failure are likely to be stagnation, political decay and, quite possibly, a return to the authoritarianism and instability of the past.

Secondly, the United States must come to terms with the contradictions in its regional strategy. Two of these, in particular, stand out: The first is the contradiction between the U.S. economic strategy and the requirements of regional political stability; the second is between U.S. counter-narcotics policies and political stability. The rapid movement towards globalization and marketization has and will continue to aggravate problems of poverty and inequality in the short-to-medium run. Privatizations of state enterprises have worsened unemployment. The reduction or elimination of tariffs have opened up Latin American economies to foreign trade and investment, often driving local producers out of business. Rapid and massive transfers of capital have led to boom-bust cycles and severe socioeconomic dislocation. At the same time, U.S. counternarcotics policies have chased traffickers from the Caribbean to Mexico and back to the Caribbean, destabilizing both areas. Successful counternarcotics campaigns in Peru and Bolivia have pushed growers north, into Colombia. Attempts to sanction the Samper administration (because of that president's complicity in accepting campaign contributions from narcotraffickers) have impaired the ability of the Colombian state to deal with guerrilla and paramilitary violence, helping accelerate the disintegration of that country.

A detailed treatment of these issues is beyond the scope of this study. The point is simply that U.S. economic and counternarcotics strategies have had unintended side effects that must be recognized and addressed. And this will require a greater degree of U.S. flexibility and imagination than we have shown so far. It makes little sense, for instance, for the United States to drastically cut economic aid to the eastern Caribbean and insist on an end to the European Union's system of preferences for the islands' bananas if the consequence is socioeconomic devastation. There is a major security problem brewing in these former British and French colonies, and it is in large part a consequence of an unfortunate combination of U.S. policies that have increased drug trafficking while simultaneously undermining the socioeconomic structures of these ministates.

In short, a rigid adherence to neoliberal economic doctrines is likely to be counterproductive. Regional security and stability will require that some protectionist structures be retained, at least in the medium run, and that the state continue to play some role in the economy (e.g., by regulating financial flows to prevent massive capital flight). At the same time, it is an exceedingly poor idea for the United States to gut its economic aid program at a time when such assistance is needed to strengthen democratic institutions and foster socioeconomic stability. As Brian Atwood, former director of the Agency for International Development, warned just prior to his departure, without a larger budget to help struggling nations, we could very well see "democracies defeated and radical leaders coming into office."[74]

Nor does it make much sense to blame Latin Americans for the failure of U.S. drug policy. Certainly, they must bear their share of the responsibility. But the driving force of the illegal narcotics industry in this hemisphere is the U.S. demand and the enormous profits generated by it. By creating this incentive, the United States has contributed mightily to the subversion and destabilization of its southern neighbors. In sum, we must clean up our own house. This means reducing domestic consumption through public health, education and law enforcement. This does not mean putting more marijuana users in jail, but hitting traffickers, money launderers and associated criminal organizations much harder. It also means imposing more rigorous surveillance and transparency on the banking system, which also increasingly profits from these illegal transactions. This must be a multinational effort to be effective. The United States should take the lead in seeking the cooperation of other states and central banks in creating an international system that would check money laundering and relieve the economic pressures on states to behave criminally.[75]

Finally, one should avoid the temptation to militarize the war against drugs. This is not to say that the U.S. military has no role. Certainly, it can support the interdiction of illegal drug shipments, train Latin American armed forces and police in appropriate strategies and tactics, plan and carry out intelligence operations and share information with them, and serve as a role model for professional behavior and the appropriate subordination of the military to civilian authority. But militarization entails serious risks and costs, and it clearly cannot "win the war." Any strategy worthy of the name must come to terms with the nonmilitary requirements of the situation. Among other things, there must be an emphasis on alternative development. This means not crop eradication or fumigation, but a serious development plan for those areas (of Colombia, Peru and Mexico, for instance) that have been largely abandoned by their countries and that have been engaged in drug trafficking for decades. The bottom line is that unless peasants are given alternative ways to make a living, spraying and eradication will just create more guerrilla recruits.[76]

In sum, a more successful counternarcotics policy will require a multifaceted strategy that will place primary emphasis on *civilian* requirements. This does not mean reducing military aid, but rather substantially increasing nonmilitary assistance. Here I am returning to the point made in my first recommendation. There is a critical need to develop Latin American civilian institutions and resources—police, justice systems, local governments, and civil society. This will require aid primarily from U.S. civilian agencies like the Department of Justice and the Agency for International Development. For this reason, it is probably a mistake to have a retired military officer as drug "czar."[77] It sends an unfortunate message. With all due respect to General McCaffrey, he is the wrong man in the wrong place for the wrong war.

A third recommendation has to do with regional economic integration. It is crucial that momentum towards a Free Trade Association of the Americas be recaptured. I do not imply by this that critics of the FTAA (and NAFTA) do not have legitimate concerns. They do. But the international balance of power is shifting, and to remain competitive with other rapidly emerging power centers (in China and East Asia, in particular) the United States will have to use its traditional geopolitical and cultural regions of influence as a motor for economic growth. And here Latin America will be very important as a source of markets, investments, raw materials and even manufactured goods. (One should not forget that out of every dollar Latin Americans spend on imports, 44 cents buy goods from the United States.)[78] Political influence and military power ultimately rest on an economic base. Unless that base is assiduously cultivated, our power and influence abroad will wane with increasing rapidity.[79] Accordingly, one of the first priorities of the next President of the United States should be the reopening of talks/negotiations with both the U.S. Congress and Latin American governments aimed at creating a Free Trade Association of the Americas.

A fourth recommendation concerns U.S. military strategy and organization. In December 1997, the National Defense Panel issued a provocative recommendation to reorganize the Unified Command Plan (UCP), eliminating the Atlantic Command and creating an Americas Command that would incorporate SOUTHCOM and a new Homeland Defense Command as subordinate commands.[80] The proposal has considerable merit. It is both comprehensive and intellectually neat. Among other things, it would bring all of the nations in the hemisphere under a single command, as opposed to the current system in which Mexico and Canada do not fall under the jurisdiction of any of the unified commands (which makes coordination between

Mexico and SOUTHCOM awkward at best and difficult at worst).[81]

Several criticisms of this proposal have been raised. Some people, for instance, argue that there is a size problem. As one SOUTHCOM official protested, this is a huge area, both in terms of geography and amount of activity. Currently, SOUTHCOM cannot keep track of all the activities in its area of responsibility (AOR). To create an even larger unified command, which would have to cope with everything that is going on in Mexico and Canada, as well as the new and ambitious mission of Homeland Defense, may be asking too much for any one CINC.[82]

Second, Mexico might well oppose the idea. As matters now stand, the Mexicans deal directly with the Joint Staff, which writes the U.S. military's Theater Engagement Plan for the country. Bypassing SOUTHCOM, with its legacy of interventions in the region, avoids rankling nationalistic sensitivities, even as it bolsters Mexican pride in having a "special relationship" with the United States. If an Americas Command meant they would have to give up that arrangement, they would be loath to do so. (On the other hand, Mexico's place within the Americas Command was not explicitly defined by the panel, and there might be room for some creative innovations.)

Third—and most important—it would be the wrong message to send to Latin America. Most Latin American militaries value their relationships with SOUTHCOM. A reduction in that organization from a unified to a subordinate command would be perceived as a demotion in the region's status. It would appear that Latin Americans were no longer important enough to the United States to merit a unified command. Coming on top of the traditional U.S. neglect of its southern neighbors and the more recent decline in resources allocated to the region, this would further undermine U.S. influence over Latin American military organizations and behavior. This would make it harder for the U.S. military to promote democratization, and could potentially have destabilizing results.

Most recently, a variant of this proposal has been developed by then Lieutenant Colonel Joseph Nuñez of the U.S. Army War College, who argues that the Americas Command should contain two subunified commands: a new North American Command as well as the existing Southern Command. Like NAFTA, the North American Command would cover Canada, the United States and Mexico. Nuñez argues that it only makes strategic sense to move from the current bilateral arrangements with Mexico and Canada to an

> organization that reflects regional economic realities and security concerns . . ., particularly considering our burgeoning trade through NAFTA and the growing threat of terrorism that can penetrate through our borders.[83]

This plan has a lot of merit. Clearly, the process of hemispheric economic integration has important security implications for counternarcotics, arms control, counterterrorism, peacekeeping, the resolution of border disputes,[84] immigration control, environmental cooperation, and other issues. While the hemispheric structures that eventually emerge are not likely to add up to a full-scale alliance like NATO, the U.S. military must adjust to the step-by-step changes that are occurring. The reality is that it makes little sense to deal with the Mexicans on a bilateral basis. It is inefficient, and advances neither their interests nor ours.[85] At the same time, however, there remain substantial political obstacles to the Nuñez proposal. The Mexicans would probably still object. Not only would they presumably lose their direct relationship with the Joint Staff, but they would be relegated to dealing with a subunified commander rather than a CINC. Moreover, such an arrangement would still send the same "wrong message" to the Latin American militaries—namely, that they are not important enough to merit a unified command.

There is, however, a third possibility. Douglas Lovelace has suggested, and I agree, that the most logical and politically acceptable approach to the problem would be to "grow" SOUTHCOM into an Americas Command.[86] Such an arrangement would avoid "demoting" SOUTHCOM to a status of a subunified command. The Latin American countries would not be isolated as the "poor neighbors to the south," but would be brought into a hemisphere-wide relationship as equals. Similarly, Mexico and Canada would be treated as peers with the United States. Everyone would benefit from the increased attention and resources that would accrue to Latin Americans by dint of their being joined with North Americans. Command Headquarters would be in Washington, DC, which would improve their access considerably. Military-to-military cooperation would be facilitated by the U.S. ability to coordinate more effectively with Mexico on issues like drug trafficking, immigration, disaster relief/humanitarian assistance, search and rescue missions, and other matters.

No arrangement, of course, will be perfect. It might still be objected that this proposal does not solve the problem of size. But that issue may be more apparent than real. There are other large unified commands—e.g., the Pacific Command—and they seem to function fairly well. Yes, there will be a lot of diplomatic responsibilities for the Commander-in-Chief. But all this really means is that he will probably have to use his deputy and staff to perform some of the functions he now handles personally. Additionally, the creation of subunified commands remains a viable option. The Nuñez proposal to have a North American Command (headquartered in Colorado Springs) could be complemented by other subunified commands for South America (HQ at SOUTHCOM's present location in Miami) and Central America and the Caribbean (HQ perhaps in Puerto Rico). Under such an arrangement, the AORs would be much more manageable than they are today.

In short, one adjusts to new circumstances. In perspective, the size argument may be more of a rationale for protecting SOUTHCOM's current status and resources than anything else. "Growing" that command into an Americas Command, with increased responsibilities and resources, would be a relatively nonthreatening and politically acceptable way to make the changes that need to be made.

A fifth recommendation concerns the need to gradually strengthen and institutionalize inter-American security cooperation. One of the peculiarities of the Latin American theater is the lack of effective alliances and enduring coalitions.[87] The consequence is that security policies tend to be ad hoc or unilateral. A crisis arises, and if Washington cannot muster multinational support for a resolution, it intervenes on its own. Institutional mechanisms need to be strengthened or created in order to discourage this tendency and deal in a more effective and multilateral manner with shared security concerns.

This is a controversial issue. Some commentators have expressed a fear that regional military and security arrangements could be used to bolster "guardian democracies" and inhibit the development of more equitable and democratic systems. In light of the traditional roles of the United States and Latin American militaries, this concern cannot be dismissed. But these critics tend to underestimate or ignore the very real security problems faced by these countries. Threats like the Colombian insurgencies and the more general problem of narco-trafficking pose continuing dangers to national and regional security and sovereignty. Unless they are dealt with, they will grow worse. When at last they can no longer be ignored, they will be much more difficult to resolve, and the costs and risks will be enormous.

The strengthening of the inter-American security system will not occur overnight. Nevertheless, it is important that a beginning be made and that Latin Americans participate. As Luis Bitencourt Emilio has observed, this is the first time they have been presented with an open agenda. There may now be an opportunity for Latin Americans to help formulate more productive security arrangements, as genuine partners of the United States rather than as objects on whom someone else's will is imposed. If they do not take advantage of the opportunity, it may pass them by.[88]

This is not the place for a detailed listing of changes that might be made. Such a compendium has already been presented elsewhere.[89] A logical place to start—and SOUTHCOM has already adopted this approach—is to foster regional cooperation under the assumption that the countries in a particular geographic area (Central America, the Caribbean, the Andean Ridge, the Southern Cone) share common problems and would be more likely to work together to resolve them. From that beginning, inter-regional linkages could be constructed, eventually culminating in hemispheric arrangements.[90]

Simultaneously, however, some changes can be made at the hemispheric level. The Organization of American States, for instance, could be strengthened considerably if it were allowed to assume a more substantive security role. Among other things, the Inter-American Defense Board could be more fully and effectively integrated into its deliberative processes. The Inter-American Defense College could be upgraded and reformed to include significant numbers of civilian students. Joint politico-military plans could be designed to cope with any number of problems, from counternarcotics to unauthorized immigration flows and natural disasters. As trust built over time, initial cooperation could be extended to increasingly substantive areas, including crisis mediation, peacekeeping, arms control, and so on.[91] Again, none of this would be quick or easy. It is the direction that matters.

Sixth and seventh, something should be said about Cuba and Colombia, two countries where U.S. policy has been not only ineffective, but counterproductive. First, Cuba: For four decades, the United States has played Goliath to Fidel's David, in the process providing the Cuban dictator with the foreign enemy he has so sorely needed to mobilize the masses behind his leadership. Castro is a master at "pushing our buttons," and we have repeatedly fallen into the trap by reacting in ways that have only strengthened the regime and contributed to its longevity. If we are serious about facilitating a transition to a post-Castro era, that should change. Rather than timidly reacting to Castro's initiatives, we should boldly launch our own.

What is needed is a strategy designed to open up the island to U.S. influence.[92] There is nothing so subversive of failed Communist regimes as democratic and materialistic values and life styles. Castro understands this far better than we, which is why he has so assiduously sought to manage and limit the economic changes that have been introduced over the past decade. In this he has been largely successful. It is one thing, however, to contain European, Canadian, and Mexican influence, quite another to limit that of the United States. The potential U.S. impact on Cuba is greater than that of any other country or combination of countries. No one else has the combination of geographic proximity, ethnic/cultural linkages, seductive standards of living, economic resources (trade, aid and investment), and strong desire to promote political change. It is time—long overdue—to begin using these resources effectively.

The place to start is with a unilateral lifting of the U.S. embargo. This should be done whether or not Castro reciprocates with concessions of his own. In the judgment of the author, such a move would be in our interest, as well as the interest of the Cuban people. It would remove the last scapegoat Castro has to deflect public discontent from his own failures. And if we played our cards right, it could begin the process of de-demonization—the elimination of the spectre of the U.S. threat—that has been so crucial to his political career. How he would react is not entirely predictable, but one anticipates it would be with suspicion and hostility. Nevertheless, it would be much more difficult for Castro to maintain popular support for his besieged fortress policy if we publicly demonstrated—in deeds as well as words—that we are not Cuba's enemy.

In short, I would argue that we should change the nature of the U.S.-Cuba "game." Fidel has mastered the politics of hostility, and we cannot effectively compete on those terms.

Only by altering the contest in a manner that he cannot fully control will we be able to exploit his weaknesses.

This being said, we should not deceive ourselves into thinking that this strategy is risk-free. One would like to promote a peaceful democratic transition and improve the human rights situation. But there are no guarantees. Castro might well react to the perceived threat to his power by intensifying repression. The transition to democracy is a slippery slope. U.S. efforts to open up Cuba might lead the regime to increase controls. It might also lead to a complete loss of control, accompanied perhaps by major violence. The latter, in particular, could produce strong political pressures within the United States for a military intervention. Accordingly, one of the tasks the next U.S. president should undertake—and the earlier the better—should be a serious cost/risk/benefit analysis of our Cuba policy.

The bottom line is that we need to determine, to the best of our ability, whether the risks and benefits of a policy change are greater or less than maintaining our current course. This can only be established (or disproven) by a more systematic and detailed examination than is possible in these pages. With this in mind, a nonpartisan presidential commission should be appointed. In addition to taking a fresh and (hopefully) objective look at the issue, such a body would lend considerable legitimacy to whatever policy emerged from its findings.

Seventh, U.S. policy is currently at a crossroads in Colombia. We have still not come to terms with the interrelationship between counternarcotics and counter-insurgency. For domestic political reasons, we have chosen to pretend that the two can be separated—that we can aid the Colombian government's counternarcotics efforts without becoming involved in counterinsurgency. But this is disingenuous. The guerrillas have become so deeply immersed in the drug business and receive such a substantial portion of their finances from it that efforts to wage the war against drugs will inevitably have a major impact on them. Indeed, this is generally understood in U.S. government circles, where counternarcotics aid is widely viewed as a way to combat the insurgency "through the back door." The calculation is that if we were candid about what we were doing the political opposition would be so great that U.S. aid to Colombia would be greatly reduced, setting back the wars against both the narcos and the guerrillas.

This may be tactically convenient, but it is also strategically insufficient. Under current U.S. policy, counter-insurgency has become hostage to counternarcotics. Partly as a result, the ability of the Colombian state to contain the guerrillas and paramilitaries has been seriously eroded. That must change. The armed forces and police must be strengthened, the tide on the battlefield turned. But while some of this can be done by providing hardware (for instance, helicopters to permit greater mobility), we must be wary of seeking purely military solutions. To fall into that trap would not only increase the death toll enormously, it could very well make the battlefield situation worse. Thus, U.S. aid should stress military reforms, training, and the development of a coherent strategy[93] more than firepower. Unless the professionalism and competence of the Colombian armed forces can be greatly improved, they are likely to use any weapons we supply in ways that violate human rights and undercut the government's legitimacy. That would be a prescription for losing the war in Washington as well as Colombia.

Gabriel Marcella and I have already offered numerous specific policy recommendations for both the military and nonmilitary facets of Colombia's "three wars."[94] Moreover, most of what I have said in previous pages about the need to strengthen civilian authority and institutions, respect human rights, reconsider counternarcotics strategy, and foster rural development is as relevant for Colombia as anywhere else, if not more so. I will not go over that ground again. One point, however, must be stressed: In its concern with the threats posed by the narcotraffickers and guerrillas, U.S. policy has neglected the paramilitaries. Yet, the latter pose the greatest security threat in Colombia today. The "paras" commit the vast majority of political killings, and their ranks are growing even more rapidly than those of the insurgents. Accordingly, a strategy must be devised for combating them. In all likelihood, the armed forces will have to play a major role. That also is why the military must be strengthened. It is simply unrealistic to expect it to simultaneously take on three formidable enemies—the guerrillas, the narcos, and the paras—in its present weakened condition. That, too, would be a formula for disaster.

The upshot is that if peace is to be attained the guerrillas and paramilitaries must be given incentives to bargain seriously. As matters now stand, they have very few. They are holding their own on the battlefield, and reaping enormous profits from their narcotics connections. There is no pressing reason why they should want to come in from the cold. Until that changes, they may be expected to use negotiations as a ploy to secure concessions from the government, while further undercutting the latter's popular support and legitimacy.

Eighth, one last recommendation may be presented in the form of a cautionary with regard to the involvement of the U.S. military in patrolling the border with Mexico. While there may be political pressure to use the armed forces to reinforce overwhelmed civilian agencies, there are good reasons why their involvement should be limited. Among other things, there is the danger of casualties. The May 1997 killing in Redford, Texas, of Esequiel Hernandez was a warning of what can happen when armed troops engage in even a passive listening and observation mode. Hernandez, a U.S. teenager who was tending his family's goat herd at the time, was shot (perhaps by accident, perhaps not) by a member of a four-man military observer team which was on the lookout for illegal immigrants and drug smugglers. The incident created a huge uproar and led to a congressional investigation. Questions were raised about the wisdom of "militarizing" the border. Put bluntly, soldiers are trained to kill enemies; they are not particularly well-equipped for the more subtle combat of border patrolling or policing. As long as armed troops are used in those or related capacities, there will be other such tragedies, with attendant casualties both civilian and military. The publicity resulting from such incidents would be damaging to the U.S. military both at the national level (in terms of its relations with Congress and the public) and in its relations with the affected border communities.[95]

To this one might add other liabilities: There is the danger that U.S. troops might become engaged in combat with Mexican units. The latter have been known to occasionally stray over the border, and it takes little imagination to envision a scenario in which there would be casualties on both sides. Even if that does not occur, the spectre of a "militarized" border touches sensitive nerves in Mexico. U.S. relations with its southern neighbor are already rife with distrust and resentment. Unnecessary provocations and risks should be avoided.

Finally, there are issues of OPSTEMPO and readiness. Over the past decade, the major armed services have steadily shrunk in both size (36 percent) and weaponry. Yet, the number of peacekeeping missions, relief efforts and other Military Operations Other Than War (MOOTW) have proliferated.[96] The services are increasingly stretched thin and can ill afford to become more heavily involved on the border. A buildup there would require the diversion of personnel from other missions and detract from military readiness.[97]

In the aftermath of the Hernandez affair, the Department of Defense cancelled armed military patrols along the border. It was the right decision and should be maintained in the future. This is not to say that the military should not provide other support services (e.g., aerial reconnaissance, personnel training, engineering, and document analysis) for U.S. law enforcement agencies. But the primary responsibility for stemming the flow of illegal immigrants and drugs must lie with civilian authorities. The military is no substitute for adequately staffed, professional, well-trained and equipped law enforcement agencies. Attempts to use it in their place merely postpone the hard decisions and commitments that are necessary if the United States is to restore the rule of law on its southern border.

On the Shaping of an Illusion and the Illusion of Shaping.

Formulating a U.S. security strategy for Latin America is a daunting task in an era of severely limited resources. For the fact is that resources shape strategy more than vice versa. Unless means are available, we are unlikely to obtain the ends desired. So we either (1) wind up with a "wish list" of goals divorced from any coherent ways of attaining them; (2) lower our goals, adjust strategy accordingly, and accept the fact that the latter is incapable of dealing with the larger challenges and dangers that will be faced; or, (3) (most worrisome) deceive ourselves into believing that the dangers do not exist or that, if they do, we can meet them with the resources and strategy at hand.

My reading of recent U.S. National Security Strategy documents[98] suggests that we are currently engaged in a combination of the first and third of these tendencies. Under the illusion of shaping the Latin American security environment, we are, by and large, shaping an illusion. Unless we can find the will to commit the necessary resources and the imagination to fashion coherent ways of linking those resources to well-defined goals, we will not really have a strategy at all. As all too often in the past, the United States will largely be relegated to the position of reacting to crises rather than preventing them. While continuing to enjoy various tactical successes, U.S. policy as a whole will be a strategic failure.

ENDNOTES

1. John A. Cope, "Hemispheric Security Relations: Remodeling the U.S. Framework for the Americas," *Strategic Forum*, National Defense University, Institute for National Strategic Studies, No. 147, September 1998, p. 1.

2. See, e.g., Max G. Manwaring and John T. Fishel, eds., *Toward Responsibility in the New World Disorder*, London: Frank Cass, 1998.

3. President William J. Clinton, *A National Security Strategy for a New Century*, Washington, DC: The White House, October 1998, p. 5.

4. *Ibid.*, p. 49.

5. Statement of General Charles E. Wilhelm, USMC, Commander-in-Chief, United States Southern Command, before the 105th Congress, Committee on Armed Services, United States Senate, March 5, 1998, p. 2.

6. See Max G. Manwaring and John T. Fishel, "Insurgency and Counter-Insurgency: Toward a New Analytical Approach," *Small Wars and Insurgencies*, Vol. 3, No. 3, Winter 1992, pp. 272-310.

7. Clinton, *A National Security Strategy for a New Century*, p. 5.

8. *Ibid.*, p. 48.

9. Barry R. McCaffrey, "A Strategy for Confronting the Nation's Drug Problem," *San Diego Tribune*, August 2, 1998.

10. Clinton, *A National Security Strategy for a New Century*, p. 6.

11. Anthony Faiola, "$1 Billion Flows Out of Brazil," *The Washington Post*, January 15, 1999; and "Unpredictable Congress Key to Brazilian Reform," *Ibid.*, January 20, 1999.

12. On the Brazilian crisis, see Kenneth Maxwell, "Brazil in Meltdown," *World Policy Journal*, Vol. 16, No. 1, Spring 1999, pp. 25-33.

13. Larry Rohter, "There's a Lot of Grit in Brazil," *New York Times*, April 23, 1999.

14. For details, see Anthony Faiola, "Deep Recession Envelops Latin America," *The Washington Post*, August 5, 1999.

15. The following is based primarily on Gabriel Marcella and Donald E. Schulz, *Colombia's Three Wars: U.S. Strategy at the Crossroads*, Carlisle, PA: Strategic Studies Institute, U.S. Army War College, March 1999.

16. During the first quarter of 1999, the economy contracted by almost 6 percent. Larry Rohter, "Colombia is Reeling, Hurt by Rebels and Economy," *New York Times*, July 18, 1999.

17. Between 1977 and 1993, per capita Gross National Income fell from US$3,310 to US$2,600. International Bank for Reconstruction and Development, *World Bank Tables 1995*, Baltimore, MD: Johns Hopkins Press, 1995, pp. 8-9.

18. Larry Rohter, "Divided Venezuela Votes on New Charter Today," *New York Times*, December 15, 1999.

19. "Now, Chavez is not Chavez! Chavez is the people! And the people will not be stopped!" Address from the balcony of the Miraflores Palace, following the Constituent Assembly elections. Anthony Faiola, "Venezuelan Leader Raises Hopes, Fears," *The Washington Post*, July 27, 1999.

20. For details, see Donald E. Schulz, "Narcopolitics in Mexico," draft manuscript, January 2000.

21. U.S. Department of State, Bureau of International Narcotics and Law Enforcement Affairs, *International Narcotics Control Strategy Reports, 1996-1999*.

22. H.G. Reza, "Drug Probes Find Smugglers in the Military," *Los Angeles Times*, December 13, 1998.

23. See, e.g., the testimony of DEA Administrator Thomas A. Constantine before the House Government Reform and Oversight Committee's National Security, International Affairs, and Criminal Justice Subcommittee, February 25, 1997, pp. 10-11; and Howard LaFranchi, "U.S. Awakes to Drug Violence Spilling North From Mexico," *Christian Science Monitor*, June 17, 1997.

24. See, especially, Donald E. Schulz, "Mexico in Crisis," *Small Wars and Insurgencies*, Vol. 6, No. 2, Autumn 1995, pp. 224-268; and M. Delal Baer, "Mexico's Coming Backlash," *Foreign Affairs*, Vol. 74, No. 4, July/August 1999, pp. 90-104.

25. *Proceso*, No. 723, September 10, 1990, p. 53.

The perfect dictatorship is not communism, not the Soviet Union, not Cuba, but Mexico, because it is a camouflaged dictatorship. It may not seem to be a dictatorship, but it has all the characteristics of dictatorship: the perpetuation, not of one person, but of an irremovable party, a party that allows sufficient space for criticism, provided such criticism serves to maintain the appearance of a democratic party, but which suppresses by all means, including the worst, whatever criticism may threaten its perpetuation in power.

26. Not unthinkable, but still unlikely, since this would probably require the PRD and PAN to unite behind a common candidate. Ideological and policy differences and the ambitions of their separate candidates have prevented this, however.

27. In November, the establishment's choice, Francisco Labastida Ochoa, defeated the Old Guard's Roberto Madrazo in the PRI's first-ever primary election. Subsequently, the Labastida camp made it a point of courting Madrazo and his followers in an effort to maintain party unity. To date, their efforts appear successful.

28. Such arguments are highly speculative. Neither case has been satisfactorily resolved. Though Raul Salinas was recently convicted of masterminding the Ruiz Massieu killing, most of the evidence was circumstantial or hearsay. Nor is his alleged motive entirely clear.

29. "Impact of Crisis 'Greater Than Expected'," *Latin American Weekly Report*, December 8, 1998, p. 570. On these issues, see Jose Antonio Ocampo, *Reforming the International Financial Architecture: Consensus and Divergence*, at *www.eclac.org.cl*.

30. For a detailed analysis, see William Greider, *One World, Ready or Not: The Manic Logic of Global Capitalism*, New York: Simon and Schuster, 1997.

31. See Cynthia McClintock, *Revolutionary Movements in Latin America: El Salvador's FMLN and Peru's Shining Path*, Washington, DC: United States Institute of Peace Press, 1999, pp. 93-155, especially p. 155.

32. An anocracy is a regime where democratic and authoritarian forms are mixed. While democratic institutions, constitutions and elections are in place, they do not function in a way in which elites are held accountable. The narcostate is one form of anocracy. See, especially, David C. Jordan, *Drug Politics: Dirty Money and Democracies*, Norman, OK: University of Oklahoma Press, 1999.

"Totalitarian democracies" are mass-based totalitarian or neototalitarian regimes epitomized by the Soviet Union, China and their imitators, and also by the Jacobin dictatorship in France. See J. L. Talmon, *The Origins of Totalitarian Democracy*, New York: Frederick A. Praeger, 1960.

33. For a detailed and insightful analysis of the weaknesses of Latin American democracy, see Howard J. Wiarda, "Consensus Found, Consensus Lost: Disjunctures in U.S. Policy Toward Latin America at the Turn of the Century," *Journal of Interamerican Studies and World Affairs*, Vol. 39, No. 1, Spring 1997, esp. pp. 15-20.

34. See, e.g., Albert R. Coll, "United States Strategic Interests in Latin America: An Assessment," in *Ibid.*, p. 56; and Institute for National Strategic Studies, *Strategic Assessment 1998: Engaging Power for Peace*, Washington, DC: National Defense University, 1998, p. 113.

35. INSS, *Strategic Assessment 1998*, pp. 112-113.

36. Caspar Weinberger and Peter Schweizer, *The Next War*, Washington, DC: Regnery Publishing, 1996, pp. 163-213.

37. Mexico's nationalistic political culture will likely serve as a major barrier to U.S. military involvement. In contrast, the Colombians seem to have comparatively few compunctions about "bringing in the gringos."

38. Diana Jean Schemo, "Congress Steps Up Aid for Colombians to Combat Drugs," *New York Times*, December 1, 1998; David Adams, "In the Thick of Colombia's Messy War," *St. Petersburg Times*, December 20, 1998. For details, see Adam Isacson and Joy Olsen, *Just the Facts: A Civilian's Guide to U.S. Defense and Security Assistance to Latin America and the Caribbean*, Washington, DC: Latin America Working Group, 1998, especially pp. 166-168.

39. This is the estimate reported by Larry Rohter, "In U.S.-Trained Force, Colombia Unites War on Rebels and Drugs," *New York Times*, July 29, 1999. However, earlier estimates have been around 200-250. See, for instance, Douglas Farah, "A Tutor to Every Army in Latin America," *The Washington Post*, July 13, 1998.

40. As of August 1999.

41. See, e.g., Coll, "United States Strategic Interests in Latin America: An Assessment," pp. 48-50; also, Stephen Blank, "The End of the Affair: Moscow and Havana, 1989-1992," in *Cuba and the Future*, Donald E. Schulz, ed., Westport, CT: Greenwood Press, p. 112.

42. See, especially, Donald E. Schulz, "Can Castro Survive?" *Journal of Interamerican Studies and World Affairs*, Vol. 35, No. 1, Spring 1993, pp. 89-118.

43. See James G. Blight, Bruce J. Allyn, and David A. Welsh, eds., *Cuba on the Brink: Castro, the Missile Crisis, and the Soviet Collapse*, New York: Pantheon Books, 1993.

44. Coll, "United States Strategic Interests in Latin America," pp. 48-49.

45. For details, see Jonathan Benjamin-Alvarado, "Cuba's Nuclear Program: A Hollow Threat?" Cuba Briefing Paper Series, No. 19, October 1998; "Pentagon Network to Track Cuban Nuclear Plant Leaks," *Washington Times*, February 1, 1999.

46. This led President Rene Preval in early 1999 to bypass Parliament and form a government by decree after more than a year and a half of political deadlock during which there was no Prime Minister.

47. See Donald E. Schulz, "Whither Haiti," *Small Wars and Insurgencies*, Vol. 7, No. 3, Winter 1996, pp. 324-359; "Haiti: Will Things Fall Apart?" *Parameters*, Vol. 27, No. 4, Winter 1997-98, pp. 73-91; and "The Challenge of Haiti's Future," in Manwaring and Fishel, eds., *Toward Responsibility in the New World Disorder*, pp. 50-71.

48. In the words of Max Manwaring: "The logic of the dialogue regarding the strategic value of the Panama Canal is simple: no threat, no strategic value. Even if there were a threat, however, there is no defense. *Ergo*, the Canal has no strategic value." "The Security of Panama and the Canal: Now and in the Future," *Journal of Interamerican Studies and World Affairs*, Vol. 35, No. 3, Fall 1993, p. 154.

49. Mark Falcoff, *Panama's Canal: What Happens When the United States Gives a Small Country What It Wants*, Washington, DC: The AEI Press, 1998, p. 66.

50. This is not universally recognized. Many Panamanians, especially, find the idea unacceptable. See the DeConcini reservation to Article V of the Neutrality Treaty, in Walter LaFeber, *The Panama Canal: The Crisis in Historical Perspective*, Oxford: Oxford University Press, 1989, p. 244; and "Do Treaties Allow U.S. to Intervene?" *Latin American Weekly Report*, July 13, 1999.

51. Gabriel Marcella argues that the U.S. presence never deterred Panamanian turmoil, and sometimes even provoked it. The latter point is certainly true, but I suspect the overall situation was more complex. I think there were crosscurrents. Whether the American presence was more stabilizing than destabilizing is, of course, impossible to prove.

52. This does not, of course, imply any intent to intervene. Continency plans are simply plans for events that conceivably *might* occur sometime in the future. SOUTHCOM is also increasingly concerned about protecting "high value assets" transiting the canal. Previously, this was not much of a problem, because the United States had forces on the ground to provide additional security. On SOUTHCOM's security concerns, see especially General Wilhelm's testimony before the Senate Foreign Relations Committee, in "Senate Foreign Relations Western Hemisphere Subcommittee Holds Hearing on Threats to Security in the Americas," FDCH Transcripts, June 22, 1999.

53. International Institute for Strategic Studies, *The Military Balance 1998/99*, London: Oxford University Press, 1998, p. 214.

54. On the Brazilian nuclear and missile programs, see Scott D. Tollefson, "Brazilian Arms Transfers, Ballistic Missiles, and Foreign Policy: The Search for Autonomy," Ph.D. dissertation, Baltimore, MD: The Johns Hopkins University, 1991.

55. Scott D. Tollefson, "Brazil's Nuclear, Space and Missile Programs: An Assessment of Capabilities and Intentions," Report Prepared for Research Sponsor, December 17, 1994, p. 32.

56. Max G. Manwaring, "Brazilian Security in the New World Disorder: Implications for Civil-Military Relations," in *Beyond Praetorianism: The Latin American Military in Transition*, Richard L. Millett and Michael Gold-Biss, eds., Miami, FL: North-South Center Press, pp. 228-231.

57. Scott D. Tollefson, "Brazil's National Security: An Overview," Report Prepared for Research Sponsor, December 17, 1994, p. 32. For a Brazilian analysis of the threats and issues that have arisen with respect to the Amazon, see Alvaro de Souza Pinheiro and Paulo Cesar Miranda de Azevedo, "A Vision of the Brazilian National Security Policy on the Amazon," Fort Leavenworth, KS: Foreign Military Studies Office, n.d. To some extent, of course, such posturing may be discounted as attempts to justify missions and claim resources.

58. Even so, funding for U.S. military activities on the Southwest Border has declined in recent years. As of FY 1998, planned funding for such activities amounted to only $105.6 million, or 13.1 percent of the DOD drug control budget, the lowest percentage and absolute amount since 1991. See Nina M. Serafino, "U.S. Military Participation in Southwest Border Drug Control: Questions and Answers," CRS Report for Congress, 98-767 F, Updated September 17, 1998, p. 5. For a critical view of the "militarization" of the border, see Carol Nagengast, "Militarizing the Border Patrol," *NACLA Report on the Americas*, Vol. 32, No. 3, November/December 1998, especially pp. 39ff.

59. See, e.g., the INSS's *Strategic Assessment 1998*; and Scott B. MacDonald and Georges A. Fauriol, *Fast Forward: Latin America on the Edge of the 21st Century*, New Brunswick, NJ: Transaction Publishers, 1997.

60. Interview with Brigadier General Ricardo Sanchez, November 1998. There is the Rio Treaty, of course. But this is more a paper alliance than anything. I mean a real (functioning) alliance, like NATO.

61. General John M. Shalikashvili, Chairman of the Joint Chiefs of Staff, *National Military Strategy of the United States: Shape, Respond, Prepare Now —A Military Strategy for a New Era*, Washington, DC: U.S. Government Printing Office, 1997.

62. General Charles E. Wilhelm, Commander-in-Chief, United States Southern Command, Posture Statement before the Senate Armed Services Committee, March 13, 1999, p. 12.

63. Sanchez interview.

64. Much, however, depends on how one defines democracy. As Thomas Carothers points out, transitions to civilian governments are not necessarily the same thing as transitions to democracy. And U.S. policy often had a negative as well as a constructive impact. For a

detailed analysis, see his *In the Name of Democracy: U.S. Policy Toward Latin America in the Reagan Years*, Berkeley: University of California Press, 1991.

65. Interview with Colonel Brett Weaver, SOUTHCOM HQ, November 1998.

66. The redesignation was made on October 1, 1999. Joint Chiefs of Staff, J-5, *Unified Command Plan For Instructional Purposes*, September 29, 1999, p. 7.

67. Wilhelm, Posture Statement, March 13, 1999, p. 13.

68. See J. Patrice McSherry, "The Emergence of 'Guardian Democracy,'" *NACLA Report on the Americas*, Vol. 32, No. 3, November-December 1998, pp. 16-24, quoted material at p. 21.

69. For a detailed analysis of the dangers of "militarization" in Mexico, see Donald E. Schulz, "Between a Rock and a Hard Place: The United States, Mexico and the Challenge of National Security," *Low Intensity Conflict and Law Enforcement*, Vol. 6, No. 3, Winter 1997, pp. 1-40.

70. Wilhelm, Posture Statement, March 13, 1999, p. 16-17. See also Ambler H. Moss, "A New Vision of U.S.-Latin American Relations" and Donald E. Schulz, "The Role of the U.S. Army in Promoting Democracy in the Americas," in *Security and Civil-Military Relations in the New World Disorder: The Use of Armed Forces in the Americas*, Max G. Manwaring, ed., Carlisle, PA: Strategic Studies Institute, 1999, pp. 40-48.

71. Coletta Youngers, as quoted in Farah, "A Tutor to Every Army in Latin America." The issue she was referring to was the use of the Pentagon's Joint Combined Exchange Training (JCET) program to conduct specialized training exercises with Latin American armies. These activities often avoided effective civilian oversight or congressional restrictions that applied to other foreign military operations. Many of these deployments seemed to go well beyond the intent of the law (which envisioned the purpose of such exercises as being primarily the training of U.S. troops) and were being used to provide counternarcotics and other kinds of training on the sly to the region's armies.

72. See the analysis of General (retired) Fred F. Woerner, "Civil-Military Relations in Latin America: Pitfalls and Prospects," in Donald E. Schulz, ed., *The Role of the Armed Forces in the Americas: Civil-Military Relations for the 21 Century*, Carlisle: Strategic Studies Institute, 1998, pp. 75-76.

73. David Passage, "Untying the Gordian Knot: Differentiating Counternarcotics From Counterinsurgency," paper presented at the conference on "Landpower and Ambiguous Warfare: The Challenge of Colombia in the 21st Century," held at the U.S. Army War College, Carlisle, PA, December 10-11, 1998, p. 3.

74. Philip Shenon, "Departing Foreign Aid Chief Says Cuts Are Dangerous," *New York Times*, July 6, 1999.

75. Jordan, *Drug Politics: Dirty Money and Democracies*, pp. 115-116. For a review of what has already been done and what still needs to be done, see *Ibid*., pp. 206-215.

76. For a more detailed discussion, see Bruce M. Bagley, "The Use of Armed Forces in Drug Interdiction: The Strategic Context," in Manwaring, ed., *Security and Civil-Military Relations in the New World Disorder*, pp. 55-62.

77. To quote Kenneth Maxwell, "a banker or a medical doctor, even a psychiatrist, would be a better choice." "Avoiding the Imperial Temptation: The United States and Latin America," *World Policy Journal*, Vol. 16, No. 3, Fall 1999, p. 66.

78. Wilhelm, Posture Statement, March 13, 1999, p. 3.

79. This of course includes our influence in the Western Hemisphere. See, e.g., my earlier comments on Brazil and MERCOSUR. For a much more detailed and comprehensive treatment of these issues as they relate to East Asia, the Middle East and other regions, see Samuel P. Huntington, *The Clash of Civilizations and the Remaking of the New World Order*, New York: Simon and Schuster, 1996.

80. For details, see *Transforming Defense: National Security in the 21st Century, Report of the National Defense Panel*, December 1997, pp. 72-73.

81. One should not infer from this that there is no cooperation between SOUTHCOM and Mexico. Actually, there is more than is

generally realized, especially with regard to intelligence and security assistance. But these are matters that U.S. and Mexican authorities prefer not to publicize, lest a nationalistic backlash set back the development of military-to-military relations. Information from several SOUTHCOM sources, including General Sanchez.

82. Sanchez interview.

83. LTC Joseph R. Nuñez, "A New United States Strategy for Mexico," Strategy Research Project, U.S. Army War College, Carlisle Barracks, April 1999, pp. 25-26.

84. While the Ecuador-Peru dispute has been temporarily resolved, it could still erupt in the future, since many Ecuadorans and Peruvians remain dissatisfied with the settlement. And of course there are other territorial disputes still simmering—most notably between Venezuela and Colombia, and the latter and Nicaragua.

85. Nuñez, conversation with the author.

86. Conversations with the author.

87. There is, of course, the Rio Treaty. But that has never amounted to much, and since the U.S. decision to support Great Britain against Argentina in the Malvinas conflict, it has become pretty much of a dead issue.

88. "Civil-Military Relations in the Americas for the 21st Century: A Latin American Perspective," in Schulz, ed., *The Role of the Armed Forces in the Americas: Civil-Military Relations for the 21st Century*, pp. 99-100.

89. See, e.g., Donald E. Schulz, "The Role of the Armed Forces in the Americas: Conclusions, Lessons, Recommendations and Unresolved Issues," in *Ibid.*, pp. 157-183.

90. Interview with Captain Randy Robb, Deputy Director, SCJ5 Policy and Strategy, U.S. Southern Command, November 1998.

91. For a more detailed discussion, see William Perry and Max Primorac, "The Inter-American Security Agenda," *Journal of Inter-American Studies and World Affairs*, Vol. 36, No. 3, Fall 1994, pp. 119-124.

92. For a more detailed strategic analysis, see Donald E. Schulz, "The United States, Cuba and the Future," *Ibid.*, Vol. 35, No. 2, Summer 1993, pp. 81-102. There have been a number of similar studies during the past decade, the most recent by the Council on Foreign Relations.

93. The current *Plan Colombia: Plan for Peace, Prosperity and the Strengthening of the State* is more of a "wish list" than a strategy connecting ends, ways and means.

94. See, especially, Gabriel Marcella and Donald E. Schulz, "War and Peace in Colombia," *Washington Quarterly*, Vol. 22, No. 3, Summer 1999, pp. 222-227, and "Colombia's Three Wars: U.S. Strategy at the Crossroads," *Strategic Review*, forthcoming January 2000. Also, Ambassador (retired) David Passage's "The U.S. and Colombia: Untying the Gordian Knot and Differentiating Counternarcotics from Counterinsurgency," revised version of a paper presented at the December 1998 conference on "Landpower and Ambiguous Warfare: The Challenge of Colombia in the 21st Century," at the U.S. Army War College, November 1999.

95. On the Hernandez case, see Amnesty International, *United States of America Human Rights Concerns in the Border Region with Mexico*, May 1998, pp. 44-47.

96. See, e.g., Steven Lee Myers, "Peace Strains the Army," *New York Times*, July 11, 1999.

97. Nina M. Serafino, "U.S. Military Participation in Southwest Border Drug Control: Questions and Answers," *CRS Report for Congress*, 98-767 F, September 17, 1998, p. 6.

98. This study covers only those recent NSS documents up through October 1998. I have read a draft of the current version, but as the final product had not been released at the time this study was completed I have not listed it in the footnotes. Nevertheless, my comments apply as readily to that document as to its predecessors.